Maths

Complete Revision Guide

Rob Kearsley Bullen

Published by BBC Active, an imprint of Educational Publishers LLP, part of the Pearson Education Group
Edinburgh Gate, Harlow, Essex CN20 2JE, England

© Rob Kearsley Bullen/BBC Worldwide, 2003

BBC logo © BBC 1996. BBC and BBC Active are trademarks of the British Broadcasting Corporation

ISBN: 978-1-4066-1369-8

Illustrations by Mathematical Composition Setters Ltd., Salisbury, England.

Printed in China GCC/01

The Publisher's policy is to use paper manufactured from sustainable forests.

First published 2003
This edition 2007

Contents

Introduction p 4

Number

Numbers and calculations

1	The decimal system	6
2	The four rules	8
3	Calculation techniques	10
4	Powers and roots	12
5	Working with negative numbers	14
6	Calculators: functions, brackets and memory	16
7	Rounding, estimating and checking	18

Fractions and percentages

8	Equivalent fractions	20
9	Improper and mixed fractions	22
10	Fraction calculations	24
11	Percentages, fractions and decimals	26
12	Fractions or percentages of an amount	28
13	Ratios	30
14	Amounts in proportion: conversion graphs	32

Algebra

Expressions, formulae and equations

15	Substitution	34
16	Simplifying expressions	36
17	Solving equations and transforming formulae	38
18	Coordinates and functions	40
19	Straight-line graphs	42

Patterns and relationships

20	Multiples, factors and primes	44
21	Number patterns and sequences	46
22	Sequences and formulae	48

Shape and space

Measurement and mensuration

23	Metric and imperial units	50
24	Time calculations	52
25	Time-based graphs	54

Shapes, angles, symmetry and mensuration

26	Angle facts	56
27	Symmetry and congruence	58
28	Triangles and quadrilaterals	60
29	Polygons	62
30	Area: rectangles and compound shapes	64
31	Area: triangles, parallelograms and trapezia	66
32	Circle calculations	68
33	Solid shapes	70
34	Volume and capacity	72
35	Similar shapes: enlargements	74

Handling data

35	Bar charts and pictograms	76
36	Pie charts	78
37	Scatter diagrams	80
38	Mode and median	82
39	Mean and range	84

Probability

40	Theoretical probability	86
41	Experimental probability	88

Using and applying maths 90

Answers 91

About *Bitesize*

The BBC revision service, KS3 *Bitesize*, is designed to help you achieve success in the KS3 National Tests.

It includes books, television programmes and a website at **www.bbc.co.uk/bitesize**

Each of these works as a separate resource, designed to help you get the best results.

The television programmes are available on video through your school or you can find out transmission times by calling **08700 100 222**.

About this book

This book is your all-in-one revision companion for the KS3 National Tests. It gives you the three things you need for successful revision:

1 every topic clearly organised and clearly explained

2 the most important facts and ideas highlighted for quick checking

3 all the practice you need.

This book contains a complete set of revision information for pupils taking the tier 4–6 tests. There are also supplementary sections for Level 7 material, indicated by: **Level 7**

The main areas of mathematics (Number, Algebra, etc.) are broken down into several topics. Each topic has a double page in the book. The format of each topic is the same, so you can find your way around easily. The features you can find in each topic are described here:

each topic is covered in two pages

copy and complete this section to build your own set of concise notes for last-minute reference

information is set out clearly in short sections

a quick check to make sure you've taken in the key points

key words and phrases are highlighted

exam questions and model answers to make sure you know how to get top marks

a reminder of the most important ideas

further practice and exam-style questions

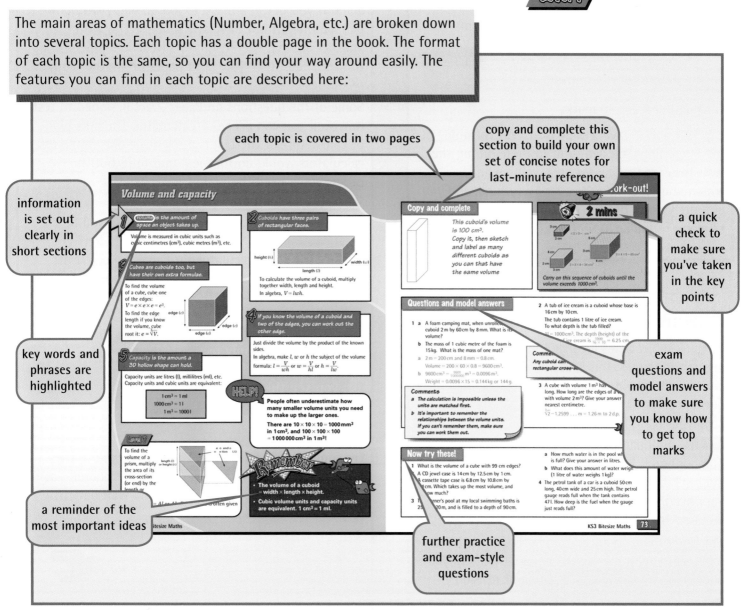

Waiting for the test to start

The tests you take in Year 9 are available in several tiers. Each tier covers three National Curriculum levels: 3–5, 4–6, 5–7 or 6–8. Your teacher will decide which is best for you, and you should know well in advance which tier test you will be taking.

The tests have three parts:

1 Paper 1 (1 hour) – calculator not allowed.

2 Paper 2 (1 hour) – calculator allowed.

Each of these papers carries a total of 60 marks.

3 Mental arithmetic (about half an hour) – calculator not allowed

This paper carries 30 marks.

Papers 1 and 2 have a page of **useful formulae** at the beginning. You can refer to these during the test. They are usually for area, volume and trigonometry, but don't cover everything, and you definitely don't get the circle formulae – so learn as many formulae as you can (see pages 58–65).

Revising maths

In many subjects, it's possible to revise by reading and making notes. This is useful in maths but you also need to get your hands dirty and do some questions. It's a bit like exercising – you need to keep your brain fit and find out your weaker areas.

Practise multiplication tables regularly. Revise number bonds by randomly choosing two- or three-digit numbers and adding or subtracting them in your head. Learn the squares and cubes of the numbers from 1–10.

One good thing about making notes for maths is that you can use a lot of diagrams. These help you be individual and creative about your revision.

Equipment

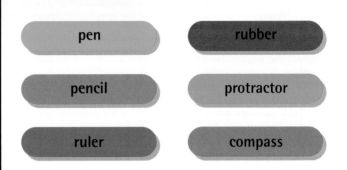

pen

rubber

pencil

protractor

ruler

compass

If you work in pencil, it's easy to rub out and start again if you get in a mess. If you go badly wrong in pen, you might not have any space left to write another answer. The invigilators (teachers supervising the test) can't give you extra paper or another copy of the test.

Some of the questions on Paper 2 are designed to test how well you can use your calculator. The best type of calculator for the test is a scientific one. Standard calculators would do for most questions but for others you'll need the extra functions on a scientific calculator.

If you look after your calculator, it should still be going strong when you take maths GCSEs. You mustn't use your calculator for Paper 1. Keep it off your desk or table, so there's no temptation!

In this book, only use a calculator where you see this icon:

For some types of question, you are allowed to use tracing paper or a mirror. The invigilators should have these available. Put your hand up and wait patiently for someone to come to you.

Waiting for the test to start

Check you have all your equipment with you and that everything is working properly.

If you have a mobile phone with you, make sure you turn it off!

You're not allowed to open your paper until told to, but you should read the information on the front cover and fill in details, such as your name and school.

During the test

Look right through the paper before you start answering questions. It's useful to know how many questions there are. The test starts with easier questions, so expect the questions to take longer as you work through the paper.

 Each time you start a new question, read it right through before you write anything. Sometimes, knowing what the later parts of a question are about can help you to answer the earlier parts.

 When you've answered all the questions (or parts of questions) you can, go back over the paper and attempt any parts you missed out. Finally, check through your answers – even at this late stage, you could correct a mistake and get yourself some extra marks!

If you don't understand a question, ask an invigilator. Put your hand up and wait for someone to come to you. The invigilators have a list of things they are allowed to tell you. If you ask something that's not on this list (e.g. how many millimetres there are in a centimetre) they can't tell you!

How the tests are marked

Your teachers have nothing to do with marking your papers. Each school has its own marker – a specially-trained teacher – who doesn't know you or any other people in your school. His or her marking is carefully checked by senior markers.

The marks from the three parts of the test (Paper 1, Paper 2, Mental arithmetic test) are added to get a total mark out of 150. Look at these mark ranges for the 4–6 tier tests.

These ranges are based on the 2002 tests. They vary slightly from year to year, but are a good guideline.

level	marks	comments
N	0–26	You can't get levels 1 or 2 on this paper – they just give you No level.
3	27–32	This is called a compensatory level 3 – it means you just missed level 4.
4	33–58	
5	59–87	
6	88–150	The maximum level available on this test.

The decimal system

1 Our system of numbers is a *decimal* system. That means it's based on *tens*.

Moving the digits of a number one place to the left makes it ten times bigger.

Each place ('position' or 'column') in a number is ten times smaller or larger than its neighbours.

A typical decimal number:

```
  3 . 2 5 1
3 2 . 5 1  ◄┘  10× bigger
```

thousands	hundreds	tens	ones	tenths	hundredths	thousandths
1	2	2	2	0	5	7

digits mean different things when they're in different places

Moving the digits two or three places to the left makes it a hundred or a thousand times bigger.

```
    3 . 2 5 1
3 2 5 . 1  ◄──  100× bigger
3 2 5 1  ◄◄──  1000× bigger
```

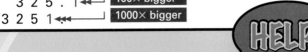

HELP!

'Twenty-five thousand and eighty-one', sounds like '2581', but there's a hidden zero in the hundreds place. It should be '25 081'.
Watch out for hidden zeros!

2 Moving the digits of a number one place to the right makes it ten times smaller.

```
6 1 . 8 8
```
10× smaller →6 . 1 8 8

Moving the digits two or three places to the right makes it a hundred or a thousand times smaller.

```
6 1 . 8 8
```
100× smaller 0 . →6 1 8 8
1000× smaller 0 . 0→6 1 8 8

3 Zeros in a number can be very important.

There is a big difference between 20, 2000 and 2 000 000! There's also a big difference between 0.6, 0.006 and 0.000 006.

However, there's no difference between 0.60, 0.6000 and 0.600 000. **Trailing** zeros in a decimal don't affect its value. The best way to write this number is just 0.6.

Leading zeros in a whole number don't affect its value. There's no difference between 03, 0003 and 000 003. The best way to write it is just 3.

Significant zeros are in the middle of a number, such as in 4.09. You must never lose these zeros as they mark empty places in the number.

4 Thousands, millions and billions allow you to construct very large numbers.

billions	millions	thousands	ones
1 2 3	4 5 6	7 8 9	0 1 2

one hundred and twenty-three billion, four hundred and fifty-six million, seven hundred and eighty-nine thousand and twelve!

Thousandths, millionths and billionths allow you to construct very small numbers.

	thousandths	millionths	billionths
0 .	1 2 3	4 5 6	7 8 9

Digits are usually divided into groups of three. This makes them easier to read.

Remember

- Neighbouring places differ by a factor of ten. So tens are next to hundreds, thousandths are next to ten thousandths, etc.

- Moving the digits of a number to the left makes it bigger. Moving them to the right makes it smaller. One place means a factor of ten, two places a hundred, etc.

Copy and complete

Digits in very large or small numbers are grouped in _____ .
Moving the digits of a number one place to the right makes it ten times _____ .
To make a number a hundred times bigger, move its digits _____ places to the _____ .

2 mins

In half a minute, write down as many different numbers as you can, using just two 2s and as many 0s as you like. In the next $1\frac{1}{2}$ minutes, write these numbers down in words.

Questions and model answers

1 Write in figures the number 'one hundred and forty-five thousand and eight'. 145 008

Comments
This kind of question could come up on the mental test. Be careful to look for hidden zeros – this number has two!

2 What number is one hundred times larger than 3.6?
360

Comments
To make the number a hundred times larger, move its digits two places to the left. So, 3 moves from the ones to the hundreds and 6 moves from the tenths to the tens. This leaves an empty ones place that has to be filled with a zero.

3 Group the digits of the number 17846370 correctly, then write it in words. 17 846 370

Seventeen million, eight hundred and forty-six thousand, three hundred and seventy

Comments
Group in threes, starting at the ones place.

Now try these!

1 Write the following numbers in figures:
   a Three thousand, four hundred and forty
   b Sixteen thousand and sixteen
   c Four hundred and twenty-five million, five hundred thousand

2 Group the digits of the number 3904000 correctly, then write it in words.

3 Aled has this number card: 0.25

His friends have these number cards:
   a Who has the card with the number

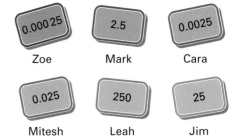

0.000 25	2.5	0.0025
Zoe	Mark	Cara
0.025	250	25
Mitesh	Leah	Jim

that is:
   i   ten times bigger than Aled's
   ii   hundred times smaller than Aled's
   iii thousand times bigger than Aled's?
   b To make a number one million times larger than Aled's, how many places to the left would the digits have to be moved?

The four rules

 The four rules of number or operations are addition, subtraction, multiplication and division.

Words and signs connected to them are:

rule or operation	words	signs
addition	add, plus, sum, total	+
subtraction	subtract, minus, take away, difference	−
multiplication	multiply, times, product	×
division	divide, share, quotient, fraction	÷ or / or −

 Knowing addition and subtraction bonds can speed up your calculations.

- You should know, for example, all the pairs of numbers that add up to 10 or 20, what is left when you take a number from 100, etc.
- Having these at your fingertips makes it much easier to do harder calculations in columns, because you don't have to work out every step from scratch.

 Here are examples of additions and subtractions done in columns.

$2145 + 629 = 2774$ $2145 - 629 = 1516$

```
    2 1 4 5            1 11 3 15
  +   6 2 9            2 1 4 5
    2 7 7 4          −   6 2 9
        1              1 5 1 6
```

 Here are examples of long multiplication and short division.

$417 \times 32 = 13\,344$

Remember that you could also use a box or rectangle method.

$4227 \div 8 = 528$ remainder 3, or $528\frac{3}{8}$

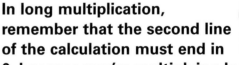 **Knowing the multiplication tables is the key to multiplying and dividing numbers.**

You use them to help you remember **division bonds**, because if you know that $6 \times 8 = 48$, you also know that $48 \div 6 = 8$ and $48 \div 8 = 6$.

 When operations are mixed up, they have to be done in the right order.

You can remember the order with the 'word' **BoDMAS**. This is explained on the right…
So $10 - 2 \times 4$ means
$10 - 8 = 2$, but
$(10 - 2) \times 4$ means $8 \times 4 = 32$.

B rackets, then
P **o** wers/roots, then
D ivision and
M ultiplication, then
A ddition and
S ubtraction

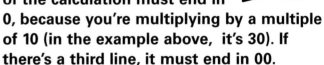

In long multiplication, remember that the second line of the calculation must end in 0, because you're multiplying by a multiple of 10 (in the example above, it's 30). If there's a third line, it must end in 00.

- Practise and learn number bonds for the four rules. They make it easier to carry out complex calculations.

- Addition and subtraction are opposites or inverses. So are multiplication and division.
- Practise pencil-and-paper methods for all four rules.
- BoDMAS controls the order in which parts of a calculation are done.

Copy and complete

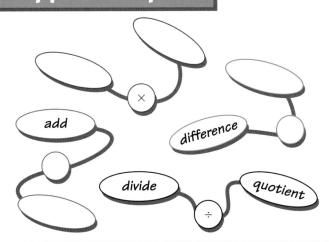

add

difference

divide

quotient

×

÷

2 mins

Copy and complete these lines:
$1 \times 2 = 2$
$2 \times 3 = 6$
$3 \times 4 = \ldots$
etc., up to $9 \times 10 =$
At the end of each line, write down what you need to add to the answer to make 100.
Now try it again, with 1×3, 2×4, etc.

Questions and model answers

1 I buy a drink costing 37 pence. What change do I get from £1? 63 pence.

Comments

This type of question can crop up in the mental arithmetic test. One way of tackling it is to round to the nearest 10p first, as if the drink cost 40p. This gives 60p change. The drink was actually 3p cheaper than that, so you get 3p more change: 63p.

2 Calculate $12 + 6 \div 2 - 3$. 12

Comments

BoDMAS states that $6 \div 2$ must be calculated first, so $12 + 6 \div 2 - 3 = 12 + 3 - 3 = 12$.

3 Multiply 631 by 48.

×	600	30	1
40	24000	1200	40
8	4800	240	8
	28800	1440	48

```
  28800
+  1440
+    48
-------
  30288
```

Comments

A box method was used to break down the calculation into smaller chunks. Notice that if you add up along the rows, you get the totals from standard long multiplication.

Now try these!

1 Use a pencil-and-paper method to answer these.
a $564 + 387$
b $2244 - 678$
c 753×64
d $5058 \div 9$

2 $4 + 2 \times 10 - 6 = ?$
For each part, write out the calculation, then add brackets so it gives the right answer.
a 54
b 18
c 12
d 24

Calculation techniques

1 To add 9 to a number, add 10, then subtract 1.

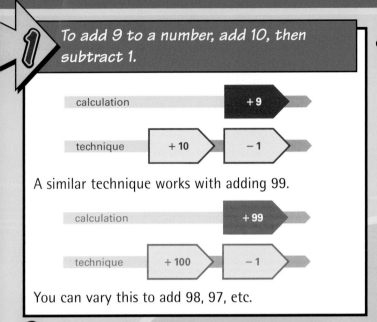

calculation   **+ 9**

technique   **+ 10**   **– 1**

A similar technique works with adding 99.

calculation   **+ 99**

technique   **+ 100**   **– 1**

You can vary this to add 98, 97, etc.

2 Subtraction techniques are the 'opposites' to those for addition.

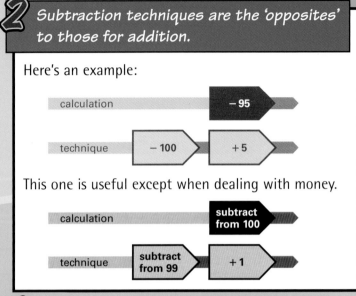

Here's an example:

calculation   **– 95**

technique   **– 100**   **+ 5**

This one is useful except when dealing with money.

calculation   **subtract from 100**

technique   **subtract from 99**   **+ 1**

3 To multiply by 10, 100 or 1000, move the digits in the number 1, 2 or 3 places to the left.

To divide, move digits to the right (see page 6).

5 Division techniques are the 'opposites' to those for multiplication.

Here's the inverse of '×20'.

calculation   **÷ 20**

technique   **halve**   **÷ 10**

HELP!

You can't reverse the technique for multiplying by 9 to get one for dividing by 9. This is because it involves the 'original number', which you can't add on because you haven't found it yet!

4 Combining operations can give you many useful multiplication techniques.

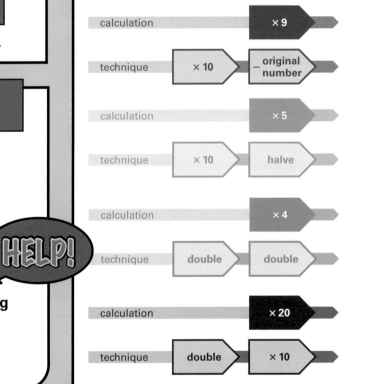

calculation   **× 9**

technique   **× 10**   **– original number**

calculation   **× 5**

technique   **× 10**   **halve**

calculation   **× 4**

technique   **double**   **double**

calculation   **× 20**

technique   **double**   **× 10**

Remember

- **Use easy multiplications and divisions (e.g. doubling/halving, multiplying/dividing by 10) to help construct calculation techniques.**

- **Jot down the answers you get along the way, but make sure it's clear which is the final answer.**

Copy and complete

Fill in the operations to match the given calculations.

Add 98:

Subtract 9:

Divide by 5:

Multiply by 40:

Multiply by 99:

Divide by 25:

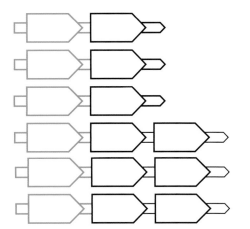

 2 mins

Starting with 7, double as many times as you can, writing down each answer. See how far you can get in 2 minutes!

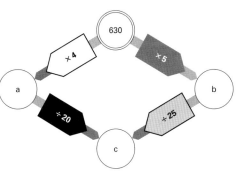

Questions and model answers

1 What is 2361 + 999?

3360

Comments

The technique is to add 1000 (3361), then subtract 1 (3360).

2 Calculate 79 × 50.

3950

Comments

Multiply by 100 (to get 7900), then halve the result (3950).

3 Divide 3788 by 4.

947

Comments

Halve 3788 to get 1894, then halve again (947).

Now try these!

1 Work out the result of each operation for the numbers in the central circle.

As there are three numbers, each part will have three answers.

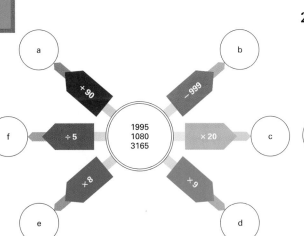

2 Find the missing numbers to complete the operation diagram.

Powers and roots

 1 When you multiply a number by itself repeatedly, you make a *power*.

In a power, there's a normal-sized number (the **base**) and a small number written up and to the right (the **index**). The index tells you how many of the base to multiply. This is known as writing a number in **index form**.

power	base	index	meaning	value
3^4	3	4	$3 \times 3 \times 3 \times 3$	81
2^6	2	6	$2 \times 2 \times 2 \times 2 \times 2 \times 2$	64

 2 Your calculator should have a power key. It will look like one of these: $\boxed{x^y}$ $\boxed{y^x}$ $\boxed{\wedge}$

Make sure you know how it works. For example, to calculate 2^6, you would probably key in $\boxed{2}$ $\boxed{x^y}$ $\boxed{6}$.

 3 Some powers have special names.

8^2 is pronounced 'eight **squared**'. 10^3 is pronounced 'ten **cubed**'. Your calculator may have special keys for squaring $\boxed{x^2}$ and cubing $\boxed{x^3}$.

 4 *Roots* are the opposite or *inverse* of powers.

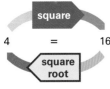 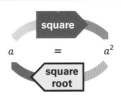 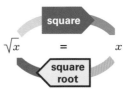

$5^3 = 125$; 125 'uncubed' is 5; 5 is the **cube root** of 125. This is written $\sqrt[3]{125} = 5$.

Each type of power has its own root. For example, $4^5 = 1024$, so $\sqrt[5]{1024} = 4$.

 5 Your calculator should have a root key. It will look like one of these: $\boxed{\sqrt[y]{\ }}$ $\boxed{\sqrt[x]{y}}$

Most calculators have a special key for square roots $\boxed{\sqrt{\ }}$.

 6 In mixed calculations, powers and roots are worked out before the other operations, but after brackets.

This is why BoDMAS has 'o' as its second letter. So 2×3^2 means 2×9, not 6^2. Your calculator should handle this automatically.

HELP! With addition and multiplication, the order of the numbers doesn't matter: $(3 + 5 = 5 + 3$ and $3 \times 5 = 5 \times 3)$.

Powers are different. $3^5 = 243$, but $5^3 = 125$! Always make sure you know which number is the base and which is the index.

Remember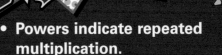

- **Powers indicate repeated multiplication.**
- **The <u>base</u> is multiplied the number of times given by the <u>index</u>.**
- **Roots are the inverses (opposites) of powers.**
- **In mixed calculations, work out powers and roots before ×, ÷, + and −, but after brackets.**

Level 7

Any number to the power 1 is just the number. So $3^1 = 3$, $10^1 = 10$, $64^1 = 64$, $1000^1 = 1000$, etc.

But any number to the power 0 is always 1. So $3^0 = 1$, $10^0 = 1$, $64^0 = 1$, $1000^0 = 1$, etc.

Copy and complete

10^2 is pronounced 'ten _____'.

4^3 is pronounced 'four _____'.

_____ are the inverses of powers.

2^5 means $2 \_\_ 2 \_\_ 2 \_\_ 2 \_\_ 2$.

In the calculation 5×10^6, the _____ is worked out first.

 2 mins

Copy and complete this table as far as '10' in the 'number' column.

number	square	cube
1	1	1
2	4	8

Questions and model answers

1 Find ⟨?⟩ in the equation $2^{⟨?⟩} = 512$.

power	2^2	2^3	2^4	2^5	2^6	2^7	2^8	2^9
value	4	8	16	32	64	128	256	512

So ⟨?⟩ = 9.

Comments

If this is a Paper 1 question, it's best to work up logically from the smaller powers. If it's on Paper 2, you can 'have a go' straight away with your calculator, trying likely values.

2 What is 7×3^3?

$7 \times 3^3 = 7 \times 27 = 189$.

Comments

Be careful not to calculate $(7 \times 3)^3 = 21^3 = 9261$!

3 What number, cubed, equals 100? Give your answer correct to 2 decimal places.

$\sqrt[3]{100} = 4.641588834 \ldots = 4.64$ to 2 d.p.

Comments

Here, you use the fact that 'cube root' is the inverse of 'cube'.

Now try these!

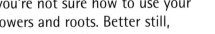

See page 12 if you're not sure how to use your calculator for powers and roots. Better still, read your calculator's manual!

1 Write in index form:

  a $4 \times 4 \times 4 \times 4$

  b $22.1 \times 22.1 \times 22.1$

  c $10 \times 10 \times 10 \times 10 \times 10 \times 10 \times 10 \times 10 \times 10$

2 Calculate powers of 11 up to 11^5.

3 Calculate the following. Round answers to 3 d.p. where necessary.

  a 5^9 **b** 100^4

  c 1.6^2 **d** 0.25^3

  e $\sqrt{2809}$ **f** $\sqrt[3]{1728}$

  g $\sqrt{50}$ **h** $\sqrt[5]{12}$

4 Find ⟨?⟩ in the equation $6^{⟨?⟩} = 46\,656$.

Working with negative numbers

You can represent positive and negative numbers on a *number line*.

As you go along the line to the **right**, the numbers get **bigger**.

As you go along the line to the **left**, the numbers get **smaller**.

2 You can use a number line to help with simple calculations.

This shows $4 - 6 = -2$.

This shows $-5 + 7 = 2$.

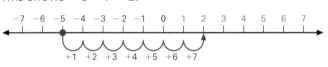

3 Adding a negative number gives the same result as subtracting a positive number.

$10 + -2 = 10 - 2 = 8$

$-4 + -8 = -4 - 8 = -12$

$6 + -11 = 6 - 11 = -5$

Subtracting a negative number is the same as adding a positive number.

$-1 - -4 = -1 + 4 = 3$

$5 - -3 = 5 + 3 = 8$

4 For multiplying and dividing, *same signs give a positive answer* **and** *opposite signs give a negative answer*.

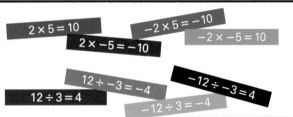

$2 \times 5 = 10$

$-2 \times 5 = -10$

$2 \times -5 = -10$

$-2 \times -5 = 10$

$12 \div -3 = -4$

$-12 \div -3 = 4$

$12 \div 3 = 4$

$-12 \div 3 = -4$

This table can help you remember.

$\times/\div$	+	−
+	+	−
−	−	+

5 The square of a negative number is *positive*.

For example, $(-5)^2 = -5 \times -5 = 25$. This means that -5, as well as 5, is a square root of 25.

6 Reversing the *order* of subtraction changes the *sign* of the answer.

$10 - 6 = 4$. This means that $6 - 10 = -4$.

$-2 - 6 = -8$, so $6 - -2 = 8$.

HELP! Be careful with the <u>meaning</u> of negative numbers in a question.

'I have −£100 in the bank,' means:

'I owe the bank £100.'

'The temperature rose to −5°C,' means just that: the temperature went up, finishing at −5°C: earlier, it was −6°C or colder.

Remember

- Adding a negative number is the same as subtracting a positive number.

- Subtracting a negative number is the same as adding a positive number.

- When multiplying and dividing, opposite signs give a negative answer.

Copy and complete

Finish labelling this number line:

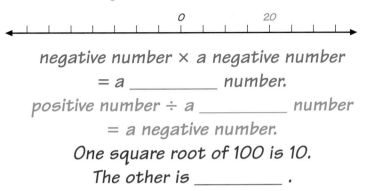

negative number × a negative number

= a _____ number.

positive number ÷ a _____ number

= a negative number.

One square root of 100 is 10.

The other is _____ .

2 mins

Write down as many pairs of integers as you can that multiply together to make -36.

Example: $1 \times -36 = -36$.

Note: integers are positive or negative whole numbers.

Questions and model answers

1 The temperature at 8 pm was 2 °C. At 4 am, it had fallen by 7 °C. What was the temperature at 4 am?
$-5\,°C$

Comments

Either count this out on a number line, or calculate that $2 - 7 = -5$ because $7 - 2 = 5$.

2 Complete this multiplication square:

×	4	−5	
−6			48
			−80
3			

×	4	−5	−8
−6	−24	30	48
10	40	−50	−80
3	12	−15	−24

Comments

First find the missing number (−8) in the key row at the top from $-6 \times ? = 48$.

Then find the missing number (10) in the key column on the left from $-8 \times ? = -80$.

Now you can find the blanks in the body of the table by straightforward multiplication.

3 Choose from the following endings to complete each sentence below:

i . . . the answer is negative

ii . . . the sign of the answer depends on the numbers involved

iii . . . the answer is always positive.

a When you divide a negative number by a positive number, . . . i

b When you square a negative number, . . . iii

c When you add a negative number to a positive number, . . . ii

Comments

a and b are obvious from the rules for multiplication and division.

To understand c, look at some examples. $10 + -8 = 2$, but $3 + -7 = -4$. The numbers decide whether the answer is positive or negative.

Now try these!

1 Copy and complete this addition square:

+		7	−12
−8			
−10			
	−12		−24

2 work out:

a 2×-6 **b** -5×-9

c $24 \div -3$ **d** $-55 \div -5$

3 a What is the square of −8?

b Write down all the square roots of 400.

4 Which is larger, -4×7 or $13 - -14$?

Calculators:
functions, brackets and memory

 1 For Paper 2 , you need a scientific or graphical calculator. Most modern calculators use *direct logic.*

This means that you key in a calculation as you would write it.

Check your **calculator's manual** to learn how to use it effectively. You will find it has many functions you don't need for KS3: you'll use more of them when you take GCSEs in two years' time! The most important ones are covered on this page.

 3 If you mis-key in the middle of a calculation, *don't start again!*

You may have an error cancelling key [CE] which allows you just to re-enter the last number. If not, you may be able to edit the calculation with cursor and delete or insert keys [◀] [▶] [▲] [▼] [DEL] [INS]

 4 You need to be able to enter negative numbers.

The key will probably look like one of these: [±] [(-)] . You **can't** usually use the normal minus key for this.

 5 You should have a power key ([x^y] , [y^x] or [∧]) and a root key ([$y^{1/x}$]).

Make sure you know how to use these. If you have special keys for square, cube, square root and cube root ([x^2] [x^3] [√] [$\sqrt[3]{}$]), these are quicker to use.

HELP! Complex calculators have many different operating modes. Some of these are no use for normal calculations. Don't get stuck in one of these modes: learn how to reset your calculator.

 2 The bracket and memory keys can help you carry out complex calculations.

Your calculator is programmed with the BoDMAS rule (see page 6), which means most calculations are done correctly.

Suppose you need to work out $\frac{7+3}{6-4}$. The answer is 5.

If you key in, [7] [+] [3] [÷] [6] [−] [4] [=] you will get the wrong answer (3.5) because the calculator does the division first. There are two ways round it:

1 use the bracket keys to force the calculator to do the addition first

2 work out the bottom of the fraction first, store it in the memory and recall it later.

Find out how your calculator's memory works:

storing	recalling	clearing the memory
[M in] [M+]	[MR]	[MC] [M in] [MR] [M−]
[STO]	[RCL]	[CLR]
[→] [A]	[A]	[0] [→] [A]

 Remember

- **Read the sections of your calculator's manual dealing with the functions above.**

- **Make sure your batteries are fresh a couple of days before the exam.**

- **If your calculator is programmable, you must delete or download your programs before the exam.**

Copy and complete

Draw the calculator keys for each function:

function	key(s)
store a number in memory	
recall a number from memory	
clear the memory	
enter a negative number	

function	key(s)
power	
root	
square	
square root	

2 mins

Work through the flowchart below.

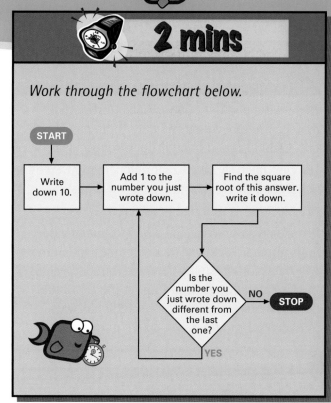

Questions and model answers

1 Evaluate $(4.2 + 8.8) \times (12.7 + 12.3)$. 325

Comments
Method 1: key the calculation exactly as it appears, using brackets.
Method 2: a work out $12.7 + 12.3$ and store this in memory
          b work out $4.2 + 8.8$ and now multiply this by the number recalled from the memory.

2 What is $-78.2 \div -0.23$? 340

Comments
Key $\boxed{(-)}\ \boxed{7}\ \boxed{8}\ \boxed{.}\ \boxed{2}\ \boxed{\div}\ \boxed{(-)}\ \boxed{0}\ \boxed{.}\ \boxed{2}\ \boxed{3}\ \boxed{=}$.
Remember that negative $\div$ negative $=$ positive, so you could work out $78.2 \div 0.23$.

3 Find the cube of 2.1. 9.261

Comments
Use the power key: $\boxed{2}\ \boxed{.}\ \boxed{1}\ \boxed{x^y}\ \boxed{3}\ \boxed{=}$
or the cube key: $\boxed{2}\ \boxed{.}\ \boxed{1}\ \boxed{x^3}$.

Now try these!

Evaluate (work out) each expression.
1 $212 \div (3.5 + 1.8)$
2 $2 \times (3 \times 7)^2$
3 $60.1 - (46 - 11.3)$
4 $\dfrac{6 + 9}{3.75 - 1.25}$
5 $3 \div (2 \div 6)$
6 $(-7)^3$
7 $\sqrt{3.1 \times (3.105 - 2.33)}$
8 $\left(\dfrac{4 \div 3}{5 \div 6}\right)^2$

1 When you round a number, you are giving a rough or approximate value for it. You can round to any power of ten.

There were about 12 000 people at a football match. You may know the gate total was 11 849, but 12 000 is good enough for a rough idea.

The first table shows 1923.8 rounded in different ways. Look carefully at the coloured digits.

Here, 6.7235 is rounded in different ways:

It's usually easy to decide which rounded value your number is closest to. Sometimes the number will be exactly halfway between rounded values. In this case, always **round up**. In the first table here, for example, 6.7235 is exactly halfway between 6.723 and 6.724, so it's rounded up.

type of rounding	nearest whole	nearest ten	nearest hundred	nearest thousand
rounded value	1924	1920	1900	2000

type of rounding	nearest whole	nearest tenth (1 d.p.)	nearest hundredth (2 d.p.)	nearest thousandth (3 d.p.)
rounded value	7	6.7	6.72	6.724

2 You can also round to a number of significant figures (s.f.).

7.1645

To round this number to 3 s.f. follow these steps.

7.16

Cover up all but the first 3 significant digits. The rounded value will be 7.16 or 7.17.

7.164

Sneak a look at the next digit. Is it 5 or above? No.

7.16

So the number doesn't round up. The rounded value is 7.16.

Level 7

You can estimate the result of a calculation.

- Round all the numbers used to 1 s.f.
- Carry out the calculation using the rounded numbers.
- Check that the result is similar to the accurate answer.

3 One way of checking the result of a calculation is by working backwards.

To check the result of $((4.15 + 6.8) \div 1.5)^2 = 53.29$, break the calculation down into steps, then reverse them, replacing each operation by its **inverse** or opposite.

forwards	4.15	+ 6.8	10.95	÷ 1.5	7.3	x^2	53.29
backwards	53.29	√	7.3	× 1.5	10.95	− 6.8	4.15

HELP!

Don't muddle up decimal places and significant figures. When rounding to a number of decimal places, count the places from the decimal point. When rounding to a number of significant figures, count the places from the first non-zero digit in the number.

Remember

- Check the type of rounding required in a question. If it's not given, choose a sensible type yourself.
- If a number is exactly halfway between two alternatives, round up.
- Check results by working backwards or by estimation.

Copy and complete

Rounding to the nearest tenth is also called rounding to _____ _____ _____ .

Rounding to two decimal places is the same as rounding to the nearest _____ .

Working backwards to check an answer means using _____ operations in the _____ order.

 2 mins

Take the number 3847.5691. Round it in as many different ways as you can. Put the results into a table.

Questions and model answers

1a Round 2156 to the nearest hundred. 2200

b Round 3.05 to 1 decimal place. 3.1

c Round 67.33 to 2 significant figures. 67

Comments

1a The nearest hundreds to 2156 are 2100 and 2200. 2156 is closer to 2200.

b 3.05 is <u>exactly</u> halfway between 3.0 and 3.1, so it rounds <u>up</u> to 3.1.

c The first two significant digits of 67.33 are 67, so this means rounding to the nearest whole number, 67.

2 Check the following calculation by working backwards: $(12 \times 0.32 - 2.15) \div 13 = 0.13$.

$0.13 \times 13 = 1.69$; $1.69 + 2.15 = 3.84$; $3.84 \div 0.32 = 12$

Comments

Writing out the intermediate answers in the original calculation gives you something to check against.

 Level 7

3 Estimate the answer to $(12 \times 0.32 - 2.15) \div 13$, by rounding to 1 s.f.

$(10 \times 0.3 - 2) \div 10 = (3 - 2) \div 10$
$= 1 \div 10$
$= 0.1$.

Comments

The estimate is quite close to the accurate answer, 0.13.

Now try these!

1 Round the following numbers to 3 significant figures.

a 89.356   **b** 275 850   **c** 0.033 05

d 1.2345   **e** 2700

2 a Check Mandy's calculation by working backwards:

$(0.57 + 0.82) \times 0.25 + 1.3 = 13.3475$

b Find the correct answer to the calculation.

c What error did Mandy make?

 Level 7

3 a Estimate the answer to the following calculation, by rounding:

$23 \times 1.87 \times 0.75 \div 15$

b Calculate the exact answer. Comment on how well it matches your estimate.

Equivalent fractions

 1 Equivalent fractions look different, but mean the same part of a whole.

$$\frac{1}{2} = \frac{2}{4} = \frac{3}{6} = \frac{4}{8} = \frac{5}{10}$$

 2 You can make a new fraction, equivalent to any given fraction, by multiplying.

- Pick any number.
- Multiply the numerator of the given fraction by your number.
- Multiply the denominator by your number.

 3 You can make equivalent fractions by dividing. This is simplifying or cancelling.

The equivalent fraction with the **smallest** possible whole 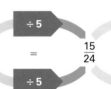 numbers is in lowest, or simplest terms ($\frac{5}{8}$ above). With lowest terms, it's easy to see how much of a whole the fraction represents.

$$\frac{2}{5} \xrightarrow{\times 2} \frac{4}{10} \xrightarrow{\times 3} \frac{12}{30} \xrightarrow{\times 10} \frac{120}{300}$$

$$\frac{75}{120} \xrightarrow{\div 5} \frac{15}{24} \xrightarrow{\div 3} \frac{5}{8}$$

 4 Numerators and denominators in a set of equivalent fractions are in a *constant ratio*.

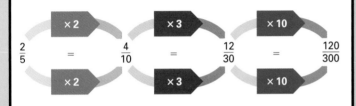

$$\frac{2}{5} \underset{\times 2.5}{\big\rangle} = \frac{4}{10} \underset{\times 2.5}{\big\rangle} = \frac{12}{30} \underset{\times 2.5}{\big\rangle} = \frac{120}{300} \underset{\times 2.5}{\big\rangle}$$

5 To sort fractions into order of size, use equivalence.

Convert all the fractions so they have the same (common) denominator, and then you can compare the numerators.

HELP!

If you have difficulty finding equivalent fractions, try making a fraction chain. Start with a fraction in lowest terms (e.g. $\frac{2}{3}$), then work like this:

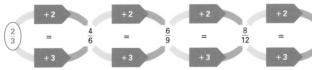

$$\frac{2}{3} \xrightarrow[+3]{+2} \frac{4}{6} \xrightarrow[+3]{+2} \frac{6}{9} \xrightarrow[+3]{+2} \frac{8}{12} \xrightarrow[+3]{+2}$$

Pick some pairs of fractions from your chain and ask yourself what number you need to multiply/divide top and bottom by to change from one to the other.

 Remember

- The bottom number in a fraction is called its <u>denominator</u>. It tells you how many equal parts to divide a whole into.
- The top number is called the <u>numerator</u>. This tells you how many of the equal parts make up the fraction.
- Fractions that are <u>equivalent</u> to each other contain different numbers, but mean the same part of a whole.
- Fractions in <u>lowest terms</u> contain the smallest possible whole numbers.

Copy and complete

Fractions that show the same part of a whole are _____ .

To find equivalent fractions, multiply or divide the _____ and _____ of a fraction by the same _____ .

A fraction that contains the smallest possible whole numbers is in _____ _____ .

It has been _____ as much as possible.

2 mins

In one minute, write down as many fractions as you can that are equivalent to $\frac{1}{4}$.

Now write down as many fractions as you can that are equivalent to $\frac{3}{10}$.

Questions and model answers

1 The fractions on these cards are all equivalent to each other. Find the missing numbers shown by question marks.

| $\frac{12}{15}$ | **a** $\frac{?}{50}$ | **b** $\frac{100}{?}$ | **c** $\frac{?}{10}$ | **d** $\frac{4}{?}$ |

a $\frac{40}{50}$ **b** $\frac{100}{125}$ **c** $\frac{8}{10}$ **d** $\frac{4}{5}$

Comments

The best way to start this is to cancel down fraction <u>a</u> to lowest terms. This gives the answer for <u>e</u>. Then you can find the rest by multiplying numerators or denominators.

2 Cancel $\frac{255}{360}$ to lowest terms. $\frac{17}{24}$

Comments

The obvious thing to do first is to cancel by 5. $255 \div 5 = 51$ and $360 \div 5 = 72$, giving 51/72. You can't cancel by 2 as only one of the numbers is even, so try the next prime number, 3. $51 \div 3 = 17$ and $72 \div 3 = 24$. This gives the answer.

3 Put the following fractions into order of size, smallest first:

$$\frac{7}{10} \quad \frac{2}{3} \quad \frac{3}{4} \quad \frac{17}{20} \quad \frac{7}{12}$$

$$\frac{7}{12}, \quad \frac{2}{3}, \quad \frac{7}{10}, \quad \frac{3}{4}, \quad \frac{17}{20}$$

Comments

Find a common denominator for the first two fractions. 10 and 3 both divide into 30. Now look at the next fraction. 4 doesn't divide in to 30 exactly, You could use $30 \times 4 = 120$, but in fact 4 divides into 60, so this is a better choice. The remaining fractions have denominators of 20 and 12, which both divide into 60, so 60 is the lowest common denominator.

Now try these!

1 The fractions in the linked circles are equivalent to each other. Find the missing numbers shown by question marks.

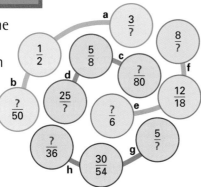

2 Cancel each fraction to lowest terms.

a $\frac{72}{96}$ **b** $\frac{132}{275}$ **c** $\frac{81}{441}$

3 Sort these fractions into order of size, smallest first:

$$\frac{1}{2} \quad \frac{7}{12} \quad \frac{5}{9} \quad \frac{7}{18} \quad \frac{5}{12}$$

Improper and mixed fractions

 1 An *improper* fraction has a larger number on the top than on the bottom.

For example, $\frac{8}{4}$ means 'eight quarters' and is equivalent to 2 wholes.

Improper fractions are also called **top-heavy fractions**. They are always greater than 1. 'Normal' fractions less than 1 are **proper fractions**.

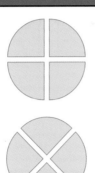

2 *Mixed numbers* or *mixed fractions* have a whole number part and a fractional part. The fractional part of a mixed number is always a *proper* fraction.

Examples:

$2\frac{1}{2}$ (two and a half),

$1\frac{1}{4}$ (one and a quarter),

$5\frac{2}{5}$ (five and two-fifths)

3 To convert a mixed number (e.g. $4\frac{2}{3}$) into an improper fraction:

- Multiply the **whole number** by the **denominator** of the fractional part ($4 \times 3 = 12$)

- Add to this the **numerator** of the fractional part ($12 + 2 = 14$).

- This gives the **numerator** of the improper fraction.

- The **denominator** of the improper fraction is the **same** as that of the mixed fraction ($\frac{14}{3}$).

4 To convert an improper fraction (e.g. $\frac{14}{5}$) into a mixed number:

- Divide the **numerator** by the **denominator**. ($14 \div 5 = 2$ remainder 4).

- The **result** of the division gives you the **whole number** part (2).

- The **remainder** gives you the **numerator** of the fractional part (4).

- The **denominator** of the mixed fraction is the **same** as that of the improper fraction ($2\frac{4}{5}$).

  HELP!

Whole numbers can always be written as improper fractions if you use 1 as the denominator. So $5 = \frac{5}{1}$, and you can then generate any equivalent fractions you need ($\frac{10}{2}$, $\frac{15}{3}$, etc.). Note that all these fractions work if you treat them as divisions, e.g. $\frac{10}{2} = 10 \div 2 = 5$.

 **Remember**

- **Improper fractions are greater than 1. Their numerators are larger than their denominators.**

- **Mixed numbers or mixed fractions are written as a whole number together with a fraction.**

- **There is an equivalent mixed number for every improper fraction, and vice versa.**

Work-out!

Copy and complete

A mixed number is made up of a _____ _____ and a _____ _____ .

Use 'bigger' or 'smaller' to fill in the table.

	proper fraction	improper fraction
numerator		
denominator		

2 mins

In one minute, convert as many of these mixed numbers as you can to improper fractions:

$2\frac{1}{2}$, $2\frac{2}{3}$, $2\frac{3}{4}$, $2\frac{4}{5}$, $2\frac{5}{6}$, ...

Change to mixed numbers:

$\frac{16}{2}$, $\frac{16}{3}$, $\frac{16}{4}$, $\frac{16}{5}$, $\frac{16}{6}$, ...

Questions and model answers

1 Change $\frac{26}{7}$ to a mixed number. $3\frac{5}{7}$

Comments
$26 \div 7 = 3$ remainder 5 ($26 = 3 \times 7 + 5$).

2 Change $4\frac{7}{8}$ into an improper fraction. $\frac{39}{8}$

Comments
$4 \times 8 = 32$: there are 32 eighths in 4 wholes.
$32 + 7 = 39$.

3 Write the following mixed numbers in order of size, smallest first:

$3\frac{13}{20}$ $2\frac{11}{16}$ $2\frac{3}{4}$ $3\frac{3}{5}$ $4\frac{1}{4}$

$2\frac{11}{16}$ $2\frac{3}{4}$ $3\frac{3}{5}$ $3\frac{13}{20}$ $4\frac{1}{4}$

Comments
First rearrange the list according to the whole number parts:
- a $2\frac{11}{16}$ b $2\frac{3}{4}$ c $3\frac{13}{20}$ d $3\frac{3}{5}$ e $4\frac{1}{4}$
- Only check the fractional parts for numbers with the same whole number part.
- $\frac{11}{16} < \frac{3}{4}$ $\left(\frac{12}{16}\right)$, so the numbers with 2 as the whole number part are in the right order.
- $\frac{13}{20} > \frac{3}{5}$ $\left(\frac{12}{20}\right)$, so the numbers with 3 as the whole number part need to be swapped.
- The numbers could all be converted to improper fractions and compared as on page 19, but this involves more work.

Now try these!

1 Match each mixed number card with an improper fraction card.

a $3\frac{1}{3}$	b $2\frac{2}{3}$
c $2\frac{3}{8}$	d $1\frac{5}{8}$
e $3\frac{1}{8}$	f $4\frac{1}{3}$

| u $\frac{13}{8}$ | v $\frac{8}{3}$ | w $\frac{13}{3}$ |
| x $\frac{25}{8}$ | y $\frac{10}{3}$ | z $\frac{19}{8}$ |

2 Cancel to lowest terms, then write as a mixed number:

a $\frac{130}{35}$
b $\frac{68}{18}$
c $\frac{216}{60}$

3 Write the fractions from question 2 in order of size, smallest first.

KS3 Bitesize Maths   **23**

Fraction calculations

1 Adding or subtracting fractions is straightforward if they have the same denominator.

Just add or subtract numerators.

So $\frac{5}{7} - \frac{3}{7} = \frac{5-3}{7} = \frac{2}{7}$

$\frac{5}{9} + \frac{8}{9} = \frac{5+8}{9} = \frac{13}{9} = 1\frac{4}{9}$

2 Use equivalent fractions when the denominators don't match.

Find a **common denominator** for the fractions. You then need to change one or all of the fractions so they have that denominator.

Follow these steps to work out $\frac{5}{6} + \frac{1}{2} - \frac{1}{4}$.

- The smallest number that 6, 2 and 4 all divide into is 12.

- 12 is the common denominator.

- Convert the fractions: $\frac{5}{6} = \frac{10}{12}$, $\frac{1}{2} = \frac{6}{12}$, $\frac{1}{4} = \frac{3}{12}$.

- Do the calculation: $\frac{10}{12} + \frac{6}{12} - \frac{3}{12} = \frac{10+6-3}{12} = \frac{13}{12}$

- Change the answer to a mixed number: $\frac{13}{12} = 1\frac{1}{12}$.

3 Subtracting a fraction from 1 is easy.

$1 - \frac{1}{4} = \frac{3}{4}$ (because $1 + 3 = 4$)

$1 - \frac{5}{12} = \frac{7}{12}$ (because $5 + 7 = 12$), etc.

4 To multiply two fractions, multiply numerators together and denominators together.

So $\frac{2}{5} \times \frac{3}{4} = \frac{2 \times 3}{5 \times 4} = \frac{6}{20} = \frac{3}{10}$ in lowest terms.

5 To divide one fraction by another, invert the dividing fraction and multiply.

Follow these steps to divide $\frac{7}{10}$ by $\frac{2}{5}$.

- $\frac{7}{10} \div \frac{2}{5} = \frac{7}{10} \times \frac{5}{2}$ (invert $\frac{2}{5}$ to get $\frac{5}{2}$ – turn it 'upside down').

- Now do the multiplication: $\frac{7 \times 5}{10 \times 2} = \frac{35}{20}$.

- Cancel $\frac{35}{20}$: divide top and bottom by 5 to get $\frac{7}{4}$.

- Change the answer to a mixed number: $\frac{7}{4} = 1\frac{3}{4}$.

6 Change mixed numbers into improper fractions.

To find $2\frac{1}{2} \times 3\frac{1}{4}$, calculate $\frac{5}{2} \times \frac{13}{4} = \frac{65}{8} = 8\frac{1}{8}$.

Change whole numbers to fractions with denominator 1, eg. $3 = \frac{3}{1}$.

With addition, whole and fractional parts can be added separately. This doesn't always work with subtraction.

HELP! It's easy to forget to change to improper fractions, and imagine that you can multiply the whole and fractional parts separately. If you try that with the last example, you get $2 \times 3 = 6$ and $\frac{1}{2} \times \frac{1}{4} = \frac{1}{8}$, giving $6\frac{1}{8}$ as the answer!

Remember

- You can only add or subtract fractions if they have the same denominator.

- Multiply tops and bottoms separately.

- To divide, invert the dividing fraction and multiply.

- Change mixed numbers to improper fractions.

Copy and complete

Fractions must have the same denominator when you _____ or _____ them.

To multiply two fractions, multiply the _____ separately and the _____ separately.

To divide one fraction by another, _____ the dividing fraction, then _____ .

 2 mins

Combine the fractions $\frac{3}{8}$ and $\frac{2}{3}$ in as many ways as you can, using the four rules. How many different answers are possible?

Questions and model answers

1 A drink is made with $\frac{1}{3}$ orange juice and $\frac{1}{4}$ mango juice. The rest is water. What fraction of the drink is water? $\frac{5}{12}$

Comments

First, work out the fraction that is juice, $\frac{1}{3} + \frac{1}{4}$. Using the common denominator 12, this is $\frac{4}{12} + \frac{3}{12} = \frac{7}{12}$.

The fraction for water is $1 - \frac{7}{12} = \frac{5}{12}$ (because $5 + 7 = 12$).

2 Calculate $2\frac{2}{3} \times \frac{3}{4} \div 4\frac{1}{2}$. $\frac{4}{9}$

Comments

First change all mixed numbers to improper fractions: $\frac{8}{3} \times \frac{3}{4} \div \frac{9}{2}$.

Do the multiplication: $\frac{8}{3} \times \frac{3}{4} = \frac{8 \times 3}{3 \times 4} = \frac{24}{12} = 2$.

Writing 2 as $\frac{2}{1}$, do the division:

$\frac{2}{1} \div \frac{9}{2} = \frac{2}{1} \times \frac{2}{9} = \frac{4}{9}$.

3 What is the square of $\frac{2}{5}$? $\frac{4}{25}$

Comments

$\left(\frac{2}{5}\right)^2$ means $\frac{2}{5} \times \frac{2}{5} = \frac{4}{25}$.

Now try these!

1 Follow the chain, working out each new answer as you go.

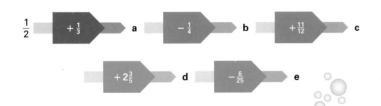

$\frac{1}{2}$ $+\frac{1}{3}$ a $-\frac{1}{4}$ b $+\frac{11}{12}$ c

$+2\frac{3}{5}$ d $-\frac{6}{25}$ e

2 For each part, multiply the fraction in the yellow triangle by each of the other fractions.

a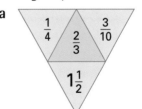

$\frac{1}{4}$ $\frac{2}{3}$ $\frac{3}{10}$ $1\frac{1}{2}$

b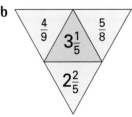

$\frac{4}{9}$ $3\frac{1}{5}$ $\frac{5}{8}$ $2\frac{2}{5}$

3 Repeat question 2, dividing the fraction in the yellow triangle by each of the other fractions.

Percentages, fractions and decimals

 1 *Fractions, decimals and percentages are equivalent.*

They all represent fractional parts of a whole. Any fraction can be written as a decimal, which can be written as a percentage, etc. For instance, $\frac{1}{2} = 0.5 = 50\%$. This also works for fractions larger than a whole: $1\frac{1}{4} = 1.25 = 125\%$.

 2 *A percentage represents a fraction with denominator of 100.*

It's simply the numerator of that fraction. So 45% means $\frac{45}{100}\left(=\frac{9}{10}\right)$.

3 *There are simple rules for changing from one form to another.*

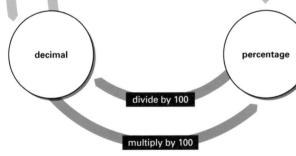

fraction

Multiply by 100.

Write as a fraction with the percentage as numerator (even if it contains a fraction) and 100 as denominator.
If necessary, multiply top and bottom to make the numerator a whole number.
Cancel down if possible.

Divide the numerator by the denominator.

Write as a fraction with the decimal as numerator and 1 as denominator.
Keep multiplying top and bottom by ten until the decimal becomes a whole number.
Cancel down if possible.

decimal

percentage

divide by 100

multiply by 100

4 *You should be able to recognise some common recurring decimals.*

Fractions with certain denominators make **recurring decimals** – the decimal has a pattern of repeating digits. The digits are marked with a dot above the digits at both ends of the repeating pattern (only one dot if it's just one repeating digit).
$\frac{1}{3} = 0.33333\ldots = 0.\dot{3}$,
$\frac{2}{3} = 0.66666\ldots = 0.\dot{6}$
$\frac{1}{6} = 166666\ldots = 0.1\dot{6}$,
$\frac{1}{7} = 0.\dot{1}4285\dot{7}$, etc

5 *To put a set of fractions, decimals and percentages in order of size, convert them all to the same form.*

Conversion to decimals is best if it's a Paper 2 question, as your calculator does this easily.

HELP!

A common mistake is to write 70% as 0.70 and 7% as 0.7! Of course, 70% does equal 0.70, but this is actually equal to 0.7 as well (see section 4 on page 4). 7% means $\frac{7}{100}$, which is 0.07.

 **Remember**

- **Fractions have equivalent decimals and percentages.**
- **A percentage is just the numerator of a fraction with denominator 100.**
- **To order fractions, decimals and percentages, convert them all to the same form.**

Copy and complete

Each number on a line represents the same fraction.
Use lowest terms where necessary.

fraction	decimal	percentage
$\frac{1}{2}$	0·5	50 % ✓
$\frac{1}{4}$	0.25	25 % ✓
$\frac{3}{4}$	0.75 ✓	75 %
$\frac{1}{5}$ 2/10	0.2	2 %
$\frac{1}{5}$	0·5	5 %
$\frac{1}{8}$	0.1	1 %
$\frac{1}{8}$	0.125	12.5 %
$\frac{1}{12}$	?	

Use your calculator to help you
write down in decimal form
the fractions $\frac{1}{7}$, $\frac{2}{7}$, etc.
What do you notice?

Questions and model answers

1 VAT is currently $17\frac{1}{2}$ %. What is this as a
fraction? $\frac{7}{40}$

Comments

$17\frac{1}{2}\% = \dfrac{17\frac{1}{2}}{100} = \dfrac{35}{200}$ (double top and bottom)

$= \frac{7}{40}$ (divide top and bottom by 5, to cancel).

2 Write the decimal 0.36 as a fraction. $\frac{9}{25}$

Comments

$0.36 = \frac{0.36}{1} = \frac{3.6}{10}$ (multiply top and bottom by 10) $= \frac{36}{100}$ (multiply top
and bottom by 10 again – the numerator is now a whole number) $= \frac{9}{25}$
(divide top and bottom by 4, to cancel).

Alternatively, you could use the place value of the decimal and say that
$0.36 = \frac{3}{10} + \frac{6}{100} = \frac{3}{10} + \frac{3}{50} = \frac{15}{50} + \frac{3}{50} = \frac{18}{50} = \frac{9}{25}$.

3 Write the following in order of size, smallest
to largest.

$\frac{7}{9}$ 74 %   0.75 $\frac{7}{10}$ 77 %

$\frac{7}{10}$ 74 %,   0.75,   77 %, $\frac{7}{9}$

Comments

Convert them all to decimal form:

$\frac{7}{9} = 7 \div 9 = 0.\dot{7}$)   74 % = 0.74

$\frac{7}{10} = 0.7$ 77 % = 0.77

The order is 0.7, 0.74, 0.75, 0.77, 0.$\dot{7}$.

Now try these!

1 Convert these fractions into decimals
and percentages.

  a $\frac{3}{10}$ **b** $\frac{9}{100}$ **c** $\frac{2}{25}$

  d $\frac{11}{20}$ **e** $\frac{5}{8}$ **f** $\frac{1}{11}$

2 Write as decimals:

  a 90 %   **b** 35 %   **c** 6 %

  d 37.5 %   **e** 110 %   **f** 235 %

3 Write these numbers in order,
smallest to largest.

  $\frac{1}{4}$ 27 % $\frac{2}{7}$ 0.235 $\frac{6}{25}$

Fractions or percentages of an amount

 To find a unit fraction of an amount, just divide by the denominator.

A unit fraction is a fraction with numerator 1.
So to find $\frac{1}{3}$ of something, divide by 3.
To find $\frac{1}{10}$, divide by 10.
To find 1 % of a quantity, divide by 100.

 To find any other fraction, divide first, then multiply by the denominator.

So to find $\frac{2}{3}$, first find $\frac{1}{3}$, then multiply by 2.
To find $\frac{7}{10}$, find $\frac{1}{10}$, then multiply by 7.
To find 45 %, find 1 %, then multiply by 45.

 If you know a fraction or percentage of an amount, you can work out the original amount.

Find the unit fraction first.
Example: if you know $\frac{7}{8}$ of an amount, divide by 7 to find $\frac{1}{8}$, then multiply by 8 to get the original amount.
If 35 % of an amount is £210,
calculate 1 % = £210 ÷ 35 = £6.
So the original amount was £600.

 To calculate a fractional or percentage increase, there are two methods.

These examples use an increase of $\frac{1}{4}$ or 25 %.

method 1	method 2
• Calculate the fraction or percentage of the amount ($\frac{1}{4}$ or 25 %). • Add this to the original amount.	• Find the **total** fraction or percentage that results from the increase: $1\frac{1}{4} = \frac{5}{4}$ or 125 % • Calculate this new fraction or percentage of the original amount.

Use the same methods for decreases as for increases.

These examples use a decrease of 20 % or $\frac{1}{5}$.

method 1	method 2
• Calculate the fraction or percentage of the amount (20 % or $\frac{1}{5}$). • Subtract this from the original amount.	• Find the **reduced** fraction or percentage that results from the decrease (80 % or $\frac{4}{5}$) • Calculate this new fraction or percentage of the original amount.

 Level 7

To reverse an increase or decrease, you must use a version of method 2.

American sales tax (a bit like our VAT) is about 10 %. Suppose a pair of jeans cost you $50.60. What was the price before tax? You can't just find 90 % of $50.60! The price you paid is 110 % (1.1 times) the pre-tax price, so you must divide by 1.1 to get $46.00.

 **Remember**

 HELP! When you calculate a fraction of a sum of money, you may end up with fractions of a penny. Remember to round the answer to the nearest penny (2 d.p. if working in £), or you may lose a mark.

- **Fractions and percentages are equivalent. The calculations used to find fractions and percentages of amounts are the same.**
- **Given a fraction or percentage of an amount, you can work backwards to find the whole amount (100 %).**
- **Method 2 above is more efficient and allows you to reverse fractional changes.**

Work-out!

Copy and complete

To find a fraction of an amount, divide by the _____ , then multiply by the _____ .
To find a percentage of an amount, divide by _____ , then multiply by the _____ .

2 mins

Calculate the following fractions of £30: $\frac{1}{2}$, $\frac{1}{3}$, $\frac{1}{5}$, $\frac{1}{10}$, $\frac{1}{12}$, 1%, 5%, 25%, $2\frac{1}{2}$%, 99%.

Questions and model answers

1 Jolene receives $\frac{1}{20}$ of a lottery win of £300. How much does she receive? £15

Comments

(note additional working for Paper 1)

To find $\frac{1}{20}$, divide by 20.
£300 ÷ 20 (= £30 ÷ 2) = £15.

2 VAT is $17\frac{1}{2}$%. Calculate the price of a pair of trainers costing £45, including VAT. £52.88

Comments

Method 1: 1% of £45 = £0.45. £0.45 × 17.5 = £7.875. £45 + £7.875 = £52.875 = £52.88 to the nearest penny.

Method 2: 100% + $17\frac{1}{2}$% = 117.5% = 1.175. £45 × 1.175 = £52.875 = £52.88 to the nearest penny.

3 Alex got 52 marks in a test and was told that this was equal to 65%. How many marks were available on the test? 80

Comments

65% = 52 marks, so 1% = 52 ÷ 65 = 0.8 marks. So 100% = 100 × 0.8 = 80 marks.

Level 7

4 A bookshop had a sale. All books were 15% off. I bought an atlas for £21.25. How much would it have been before the sale? £25.00

Comments

15% off means that all books cost 85% of what they did originally. Their prices have been multiplied by 0.85. So the pre-sale price was £21.25 ÷ 0.85 = £25.00.

Now try these!

1 Alannah puts 6% of her salary into a pension fund. She earns £17 000 per year. How much goes into the fund each year?

2 A packet contains 500 flower seeds. 40% of the seeds will grow red flowers and 60%, orange flowers. How many of each type are in the packet?

3 $\frac{3}{8}$ of a cake is left. This weighs 240 grams. How much did the whole cake weigh?

4 John's car cost £8500 new. Its value has decreased by 12%. What is it worth now?

5 The cost of a rail ticket this year is £55. This is due to rise by 5%. What will it cost after the rise?

Level 7

6 The cost of a console game after VAT ($17\frac{1}{2}$%) is added is £39.99. What was the price without VAT?

Ratios

1 Ratios allow you to compare numbers or amounts.

Suppose there's a class of 28 pupils, 8 of whom are girls.

20 boys and 8 girls
boys : girls = **20 : 8**

10 boys to every 4 girls
boys : girls = **10 : 4**

5 boys to every 2 girls
boys : girls = **5 : 2**

All these ratios are **equivalent**. The ratio 5:2 is in its **lowest terms**.

You can make equivalent ratios in a similar way to how you make equivalent fractions: multiply or divide all parts of the ratio by the same number.

3 Unlike fractions, ratios can have more than two parts.

For example, you could share out £200 between three people in the ratio 5:4:1. There are
5 + 4 + 1 = 10 'shares', so each 'share' is £20. The money is divided in the ratio £100:£80:£20.

| 5 | : | 4 | : | 1 |

2 Unitary ratios contain the number 1.

In the class example in section 1, the unitary ratios are:
- divide both sides of 5:2 by 2
  boys: girls = **2.5 : 1**
  (there are 2.5 boys to every girl)
- divide both sides of 5:2 by 5
  boys: girls = **1 : 0.4**
  (there are 0.4 girls to every boy)

4 Maps, scale drawings and models use ratios to tell you their scale.

The ratio is always given as scale size : actual size.

A 1:32 scale model of a boat is $\frac{1}{32}$ the actual size of the boat.

Features on a map drawn at 1:25 000 are $\frac{1}{25\,000}$ of their actual size.

A diagram of a circuit on a scale of 20:1 is 20 times **larger** than the real thing.

Some people forget that the total of the numbers in a ratio can be important. For example, if an orange drink is made with juice and water in the ratio 1:5, the drink is <u>not</u> $\frac{1}{5}$ juice. It's $\frac{1}{6}$, as there are 6 parts altogether in the mixture.

- Ratios compare amounts in this way: 'so many of this to every so many of that'.
- Several ratios containing different numbers may be equivalent.
- Unitary ratios contain the number 1.
- The scale of a map, scale drawing or scale model is expressed as a ratio.

Copy and complete

A ratio containing the smallest possible whole numbers is in _____ _____ .

A ratio in which one of the parts is 1 is called a _____ ratio.

A scale drawing on a scale of 1:10 is 10 times _____ than the real thing.

Create equivalent ratios by _____ or _____ all parts of the ratio by the same number.

2 mins

Write down five different two-part ratios.

Write each of them in the form $1:m$ and $n:1$. Look at the values of m and n. Is there any connection between them?

Questions and model answers

1 Write the ratio 30:48

   a in lowest terms

   b in the form $1:m$, where m is a decimal number

   c in the form $n:1$, where n is a decimal number.

   a 5:8   *(divide 30 and 48 by 6)*

   b 1:1.6   *(divide 5 and 8 by 5)*

   c 0.625:1   *(divide 5 and 8 by 8)*

2 The scale of a map is 1:1250. Andie measures the distance from her house to school on the map as 24 cm. How far is it really?

   300 metres or 0.3 km

3 In a fruit cake, the ratio of currants : sultanas : cherries = 7 : 4 : 1. Mamie used 420 g of currants. How much fruit did she use altogether, and how much of the other ingredients did she use?

   720 g fruit altogether, 240 g sultanas, 60 g cherries.

Comments

7 + 4 + 1 = 12, so there are 12 'shares' in the fruit mix. 1 'share' = 420 g ÷ 7 = 60 g.

12 × 60 g = 720 g, 4 × 60 g = 240 g and 1 × 60 g = 60 g.

Comments

Multiply map distances by 1250 to find real distances. 24 × 1250 = 30 000 cm = 300 m.

Now try these!

1 All the ratios below are equivalent to 8:12. Find the missing numbers.

   a 2:☐   **b** 1:☐   **c** ☐:15

   d 50:☐   **e** ☐:36

2 In a traffic survey, the vehicles on a motorway were found to be in the ratio cars : trucks : buses = 4 : 2 : 1.

2100 vehicles were surveyed. How many of each type were there?

3 A scale model of a car is 15 cm long. The real car is 3 m long. What is the scale of the model?

4 Landranger maps are on a scale of 1:50 000. A section of railway is 12 km long. How long does it appear on the map?

Amounts in proportion: conversion graphs

1 Two amounts that stay in the same ratio to each other are said to be *in proportion*.

For example, a recipe needs 50 g of rice for each person, so the ratio persons : grams of rice = 1 : 50, always. The number of persons and the weight of rice are **proportional** to each other.

One amount is a fixed **multiple** of the other.

2 If you multiply or divide one of the proportional quantities by a number, you *must* do the same to the other.

For example, if 10 litres of petrol cost £7, 20 litres will cost double, £14, and 5 litres will cost half, £3.50. This **doesn't** work with addition or subtraction!

3 Use the *unitary method* when calculating with proportional amounts.

Example: 12 identical pieces of model railway track stretch for 3.84 m. How far will 10 pieces stretch?

The **unitary method** involves finding the length of 1 piece.

    12 pieces = 3.84 m

    1 piece = 3.84 ÷ 12 = 0.32 m

    10 pieces = 0.32 × 10 = **3.2 m**

Suppose you needed to know how many pieces would be needed for 5 m of track.

    3.84 m = 12 pieces

    1 m = 12 ÷ 3.84 = 3.125 pieces

    5 m = 5 × 3.125 = 15.625 pieces

    So to stretch 5 m, **16 pieces** are needed.

4 If you plot two proportional amounts against each other on a graph, you get a *straight line through the origin*.

Here's a graph illustrating the rice recipe.

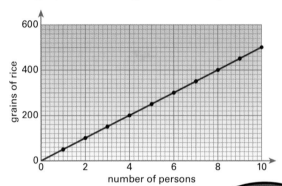

HELP!

When reading information from a conversion graph, be careful to start at the correct axis. Where the ranges of values on the axes are similar, it's easy to get mixed up.

5 *Conversion graphs* connect two proportional quantities.

As an example, this graph converts between pounds and euros.

The red line shows that £40 is worth about 67 euros (it's impossible to be more accurate without a bigger scale).

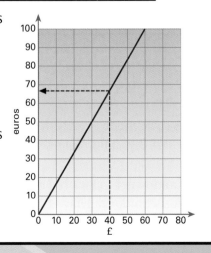

Remember

- **Proportional amounts are in a fixed ratio. One is a fixed multiple of the other. If one amount is multiplied or divided by a number, the other must be too.**

- **Proportional amounts plotted on a graph make a straight line through the origin.**

Copy and complete

Two amounts that are in a fixed ratio are said to be in _____ .
When proportional amounts are plotted against each other, the graph is a _____ _____ through the _____ .

2 mins

X and Y are proportional quantities. Copy and complete this table.

X			12	15	30	
Y	2	3	5			17.5

Questions and model answers

1 Are the two quantities A and B in proportion? If so, what is the ratio $A:B$, in unitary form?

A	2	5	6	10	25
B	5	7.5	15	25	62.5

What is the value of A when $B = 10$?
Yes, A and B are in proportion.
$A:B = 1:2.5$ or $0.4:1$. When $B = 10$, $A = 4$.

Comments

Just divide all the B values by their A values. You should always get 2.5. If you do it the other way round, you should always get 0.4.
$A:B = 2:5$, which by division is $1:2.5$ or $0.4:1$.
$B \div A = 2.5$, so $10 \div A = 2.5$, so $A = 4$.

Now try these!

1 a From the table in the '2 mins' section, what is the ratio $X:Y$, in the form $m:1$?
   b On graph paper, plot X against Y.
   c Use your graph to find the value of Y, when $X = 10$.

2 A building mixture uses sand, cement and water in the ratio $6:3:1$. Mitesh has 45 kg of sand.
   a How much of the other ingredients does he need?
   b How much mixture can he make?

3 16 pencils cost £1.92. How much do 20 cost?

2 A meal for 4 people needs 500 g of potatoes.
   a What weight of potatoes is needed for 7 people?
   a 4 people = 500 g
      1 person = 500 g ÷ 4 = 125 g
      7 people = 125 g × 7 = 875 g
   b How many people could eat this meal if it were made with 1200 g potatoes?
   b 500 g = 4 people
      100 g = 4 ÷ 5 = 0.8 people
      1200 g = 12 × 0.8 = 9.6 people
      There would be enough for 9 people, but not 10.

Comments

Note that in b, it's not necessary to work out the value for 1 g of potato – work in 'units' of 100 g.

3 A stationery shop sells coloured paper by weight. Use the graph to find:

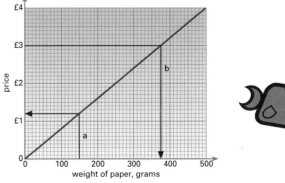

a the cost of 150 g of paper £1.20
b how much paper can be bought for £3. 375 g

Substitution

 1 In algebra, *expressions* contain one or more *terms*.

Terms contain letters and numbers connected by multiplication, division, powers or roots.

These are all terms:

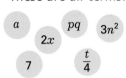
a $2x$ pq $3n^2$ 7 $\frac{t}{4}$

You combine terms using addition and subtraction to make **expressions**. For example, $a + 2x - \frac{t}{4}$ is an expression with three terms.

 2 Multiplication signs aren't used in terms and expressions.

So $2x$ means $2 \times$ the number x, and pq means $p \times q$.
Division is usually written in fraction style, so $t \div 4$ becomes $\frac{t}{4}$.

 3 When you are given *values* for the letters in an expression, you can *evaluate* it.

Work out the value of an expression by **substituting** numbers for the letters in it. Follow the usual BoDMAS rules (page 6, section 6).

For example, if $d = 5$,
then $3d - 2 = 3 \times 5 - 2 = 15 - 2 = 13$.
However, $3(d - 2) = 3(5 - 2) = 3 \times 3 = 9$.

4 A *formula* is like a set of instructions for working something out.

It has a **subject** (what's being worked out), usually on the left of the equals sign. On the other side is an expression containing the instructions. For example, the perimeter (P) of this hexagon is given by $P = 2a + 4b$. As you substitute different values for a and b, you get different-shaped hexagons, and different perimeters.

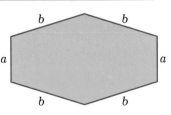

If $a = 6$ cm and $b = 10$ cm, then
$P = 2a + 4b = 2 \times 6 + 4 \times 10 = 12 + 40 = 52$ cm.

 5 You may be asked to construct a formula to match a set of instructions.

You may be given the letters to use, or you may be able to choose your own.

For example, here's a rough way of working out the stopping distance (d metres) for a car travelling at v miles per hour:

Square the speed.	v^2
Add 10 times the speed to this.	$v^2 + 10v$
Divide the total by 60.	$\frac{v^2 + 10v}{60}$

So the formula is $d = \dfrac{v^2 + 10v}{60}$.

 HELP! When substituting in a multiplication, don't forget to put the multiplication sign back.

If $x = 3$, $2x$ means 2×3, not 23!

 **Remember**

- **Evaluate an expression by substituting numbers for letters.**

- **Multiplication signs aren't used in algebra, but must be put back in when you substitute.**

- **A formula has a subject, an equals sign and an expression that tells you how to calculate the subject.**

Copy and complete

A formula tells you how to calculate something, the _____ of the formula. When you substitute into an expression, you replace _____ by their _____ .

Copy and complete this table.

x	-2	-1	0	1	2
x^2				1	
$3x$				3	
$x^2 - 3x$				-2	

Questions and model answers

1 $a = 3$, $b = 10$ and $p = 4$. Find the value of

  a $4a + 5$ **b** $4(a + 5)$

  c pb^2 **d** $(pb)^2$

  a $4a + 5 = 4 \times 3 + 5 = 12 + 5 = \mathbf{17}$

  b $4(a + 5) = 4(3 + 5) = 4 \times 8 = \mathbf{32}$

  c $pb^2 = 4 \times 10^2 = 4 \times 100 = \mathbf{400}$

  d $(pb)^2 = (4 \times 10)^2 = 40^2 = \mathbf{1600}$

2 The perimeter of a rectangle (P) with length l and width w is calculated as follows.

  • Add the length and width together.

  • Double the result.

  a Write a formula for the perimeter.

  b Use your formula to calculate the perimeter of a rectangle 31 m long by 18.5 m wide.

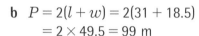

  a $P = 2(l + w)$

  b $P = 2(l + w) = 2(31 + 18.5)$
       $= 2 \times 49.5 = 99$ m

Comments

Be careful not to work out $2l + w$ by mistake.

3 What is the value of $10 - 2h$, when $h = -3$?

  $10 - 2h = 10 - 2 \times -3$
         $= 10 - -6 = 10 + 6 = 16$

Comments

Care needs to be taken when substituting negative numbers. No signs should be lost.

Now try these!

1 Find the value of $\dfrac{a + b}{2c}$ when:

  a $a = 2$, $b = 6$ and $c = 1$.

  b $a = 5$, $b = 5$ and $c = 5$.

  c $a = 0.1$, $b = 0.3$ and $c = 0.05$.

  d $a = -10$, $b = -8$ and $c = -6$.

2 The cost, C pence, of a call on a telephone network is calculated from the length, t seconds, of the call.

  • Add 30 to the length of the call.

  • Divide the result by 20.

  a Write down a formula based on the information above.

  b Use this to calculate the cost of a **3-minute** call.

3 If n is a number, write down an expression for each of these:

  a one more than the number.

  b twice the number.

  c four times the number, taken away from ten.

  d one hundred, divided by the number.

Simplifying expressions

 1 *Like terms are terms that contain the same letter or combination of letters.*

Each cloud contains terms that are **like** each other.

- a, $10a$, $2a$, $-5a$
- pq, $-pq$, $3pq$, qp
- x^2, $9x^2$, $-x^2$

 2 Terms containing different powers of the same letter are **not** like terms.

So n, n^2, n^3 and $\frac{1}{n}$ are not like terms. They are called **unlike** terms.

 3 *Like terms can be collected together and simplified.*

$$a + 2a + 3a = 6a$$
$$4xy - xy = 3xy$$

 4 Sometimes different types of terms are mixed up together.

You can simplify these by **grouping** the like terms together first.
$2p + 4q + 5p - 6q$
is the same as
$2p + 5p + 4q - 6q$,
which simplifies to $7p - 2q$

 5 *A bracket containing terms can be multiplied by a number or letter.*

When this happens, you can **expand**, multiplying each term in the bracket by the number outside.
Examples: $3(4u + 5) = 12u + 15$
$n(x + y) = nx + ny$

 Level 7

To multiply two brackets of the form $(x + n)$ together, split the first one, as follows.
Expand $(x + 8)(x + 4)$: Split the first bracket to get
$x(x + 4) + 8(x + 4) = x^2 + 4x + 8x + 32$.
Finally, collect x terms to get $x^2 + 12x + 32$.

6 *Sometimes you can expand and simplify.*

$$
\begin{aligned}
2(3h - 4k) - 3(h + 2k) &= 6h - 8k - 3h - 6k \\
&= 6h - 3h - 8k - 6k \\
&= 3h - 14k
\end{aligned}
$$

(note the $-$ signs from the 2nd bracket)
(keep the $-$ signs with their terms)

 **Remember**

HELP!

Be very careful with minus signs when multiplying and when grouping terms.

It's easy to lose a sign, especially when multiplying a bracket by a negative number.

- **Like terms contain the same combination of letters.**
- **Collect like terms to simplify an expression.**
- **Expand a bracket by multiplying every term inside it.**

Copy and complete

If terms contain the same combination of letters, they are _____ terms.
If not, they are _____ .
To simplify an expression, _____ brackets and _____ like terms.

2 mins

Explain why uv and vu are like terms, but $\frac{u}{v}$ and $\frac{v}{u}$ are not.

Questions and model answers

1 Simplify the following expression:
$2r + 3s - 5r + 6s + r$.

$$2r + 3s - 5r + 6s + r = 2r - 5r + r + 3s + 6s$$
$$= -2r + 9s$$

Comments

The answer $9s - 2r$ is also fine. You can re-order the terms so the final expression starts with a positive number.

2 Expand and simplify $3(z - 4) + 2(2z + 7)$.
$$3(z - 4) + 2(2z + 7) = 3z - 12 + 4z + 14$$
$$= 3z + 4z - 12 + 14$$
$$= 7z + 2$$

Comments

If you can collect the like terms without writing out the rearrangement, this is OK.

3 Simplify $1 + n + 2n^2 - 3n + 2$.
$$1 + n + 2n^2 - 3n + 2 = 1 + 2 + n - 3n + 2n^2$$
$$= 3 - 2n + 2n^2$$

Comments

It is usual to write terms like this starting with the largest power. This would give $2n^2 - 2n + 3$.

Now try these!

1 Simplify the following expressions, expanding brackets where necessary.

  a $j + k + 2j + 6k$ **b** $3e - 3d - e + 2d$

  c $4y + 9 - 7y - 3$ **d** $2(w + 8)$

  e $b(b + 1)$ **f** $3(T + 8) + 2(2T + 1)$

  g $2(4x + y) - (x - y)$ **h** $6(2g - 2h) + 5(g + 3h)$

2 N is a whole number.

  a Write an expression for the next whole number, counting on from N.

  b Write an expression for the next whole number after that.

  c Write an expression for the sum of N and its two 'next numbers'.

  d Simplify your expression.

  e Explain why this sum must be a multiple of 3.

3 Expand and simplify:

  a $(x + 5)(x + 2)$

  b $(x + 6)(x - 1)$

Solving equations
and transforming formulae

1 An *equation* is a puzzle to be solved.

Equations contain an unknown number, often x. Finding the value of x is called **solving** the equation. The value of x is the **solution**. On this page, there are two methods of solving $5x + 6 = 10$. Think of the equation as 'I'm thinking of a number. If you multiply it by 5, then add 6, you get 10. What's my number?'

3 You can solve equations by rearranging the algebra.

Always do the same thing to both sides:

$5x + 6 = 10$	*(write down the equation)*
$5x = 10 - 6$	*(subtract 6 from both sides)*
$5x = 4$	*(simplify)*
$x = 4 \div 5$	*(divide both sides by 5)*
$x = 0.8$	*(simplify: that's the solution)*

5 Changing the subject of a formula is very like solving an equation.

Suppose you have the formula $P = 2a + 4b$, and you want a formula that calculates b, if you know P and a. Swap the two sides of the equation so the expression containing b is on the left, then:

$2a + 4b = P$	
$4b = P - 2a$	*(subtract 2a from both sides)*
$b = \dfrac{P - 2a}{4}$	*(divide both sides by 4)*

6 Sometimes you're allowed to guess the solution!

You can find an **approximate solution** to more complicated equations by **trial and improvement**.

Try out a value for x, then use the result to make a better guess. For example, to find the value of x that solves $x^2 + 2x = 10$, you might try $x = 1, 2, 3, 2.5, 2.4, 2.3, 2.31, 2.32, 2.315$. Substitute these values yourself and try to work out why they were chosen.

2 Solve simple equations by 'working backwards' with number machines.

To work backwards, turn the number machines round and use the inverse operations.

$10 - 6 = 4$; $4 \div 5 = 0.8$. The solution is $x = 0.8$.
(Check by substituting 0.8 for x in the first set of number machines.)

4 For more complex equations, you must use rearrangement.

Here, the unknown is on both sides of the equation.

$4x - 5 = 2x - 3$	*(write down the equation)*
$4x - 2x - 5 = -3$	*(subtract 2x from both sides)*
$2x - 5 = -3$	*(simplify)*
$2x = -3 + 5$	*(add 5 to both sides)*
$2x = 2$	*(simplify)*
$x = 1$	*(divide both sides by 2: that's the solution)*

Expand any brackets and simplify expressions as much as possible before solving the equation.

- **Solve equations by working backwards through a sequence of operations, or by rearranging and simplifying.**

- **Expand brackets and simplify expressions as much as possible before solving.**

- **Use trial and improvement where the solution can't be found exactly.**

- **Rearrange formulae in the same way as you would solve equations.**

Copy and complete

To solve an equation, _____ and _____ it as much as possible, then apply _____ operations in the _____ order.

2 mins

Write down as many equations as you can that have the solution $x = 2$.

Questions and model answers

1 Solve $4x + 3 = 1$.

Using number machines

gives the following method to work backwards:

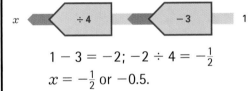

$1 - 3 = -2; \ -2 \div 4 = -\frac{1}{2}$

$x = -\frac{1}{2}$ or -0.5.

2 Solve $2(x + 5) = 3(2x - 4)$.

$2(x + 5) = 3(2x - 4)$	(write out the equation)
$2x + 10 = 6x - 12$	(expand brackets on both sides)
$2x - 6x + 10 = -12$	(subtract $6x$ from both sides)
$-4x + 10 = -12$	(simplify on the left)
$-4x = -12 - 10$	(subtract 10 from both sides)
$-4x = -22$	(simplify on the right)
$4x = 22$	(multiply both sides by -1)
$x = 22 \div 4$	(divide both sides by 4)
$x = 5.5$	(simplify on the right)

Comments

You need to be careful using negative numbers.

3 Show that there is a solution of $x^3 - 5x = 1$, between $x = 2$ and $x = 3$. Find this solution correct to 1 d.p. $x = 2.3$

Comments

Note that once you know x is between 2.3 and 2.4, you need to check 2.35 to see which of them it's closer to.

x	$x^3 - 5x$	Comments
2	-2	Too small.
3	12	Too big. The solution is somewhere between $x = 2$ and $x = 3$.
2.5	3.125	Try halfway between 2 and 3. Too big. x must be less than this.
2.2	-0.352	Too small.
2.3	0.667	Still too small.
2.4	1.824	Too big; x is between 2.3 and 2.4.
2.35	1.227875	Too big; x is between 2.3 and 2.35.

Now try these!

1 Solve the following equations.

  a $2x + 8 = 14$ **b** $3x + 4 = 1$

  c $5x - 3 = x + 7$ **d** $11 - 2x = 8$

  e $4(2x + 1) = 20$

2 a Make y the subject of $x - 2y = 4$.

  b Make w the subject of $P = 2(l + w)$.

3 a Show that there is a solution of $x^2 - 4x = 2$ between $x = 4$ and $x = 5$.

  b Find the solution, correct to 2 d.p.

Coordinates and functions

 A *function* is a set of mathematical instructions. Functions can be described using algebra.

A function acts on a set of numbers (**inputs**) to produce a new set of numbers (**outputs**). This is called a **mapping**. The function **maps** the input numbers to the output numbers.

For example, a simple function is 'double the input'. This maps the set {1, 2, 3, 4, 5} to {2, 4, 6, 8, 10}. Using the letter x for the input, the function 'double the input' will produce $2x$ as its output. This is written as $x \longrightarrow 2x$.

 A *mapping diagram* shows all the features of a mapping.

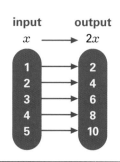

 Mappings can also be represented on a coordinate grid.

Use the x-axis for the inputs and the y-axis for the outputs. The function can be written using an equation: $y = 2x$.

This makes sense, because the y-coordinate of each point marked on the graph is double its x-coordinate.

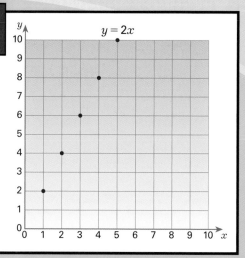

HELP!

When plotting coordinates, don't forget that:

- the x-value gives the number of grid units left or right from the origin
- the y-value gives the number up or down from the origin.

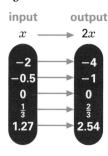 Functions don't just work on whole numbers.

You could use anything you like as the input: fractions, decimals, negative numbers, etc. These 'fill up the gaps' between the points on the grid and turn the pattern into a straight line. Here's a mapping diagram for $x \longrightarrow 2x$, with different inputs, and the finished graph of $y = 2x$.

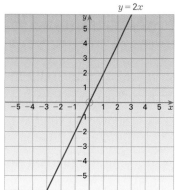

Remember

- A function takes input numbers and maps them to its output numbers.
- Mapping diagrams and coordinate grids can be used to show the results of mappings.
- Functions can be described with algebra.

Copy and complete

In a mapping, a _____ acts on _____ numbers to produce _____ numbers.

Write down, using algebra, as many functions as you can that give output 1 from an input of 0.

Questions and model answers

1 What is the output set produced by the function $x \rightarrow 10 - x^2$, acting on the input set $\{-1, 0, 1, 2, 3\}$?

$\{9, 10, 9, 6, 1\}$

Comments

Remember that the square of a negative number is positive, ie. $(-1)^2 = 1$.

2 Describe the following mapping using algebra: $x \rightarrow 6 - x$ or $y = 6 - x$.

Comments

If you notice that the input and output numbers always add up to 6, you could write this as $x + y = 6$, then make y the subject.

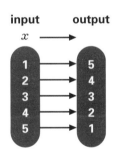

3

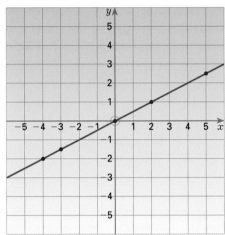

Copy and complete the mapping diagram for the function shown on this graph.

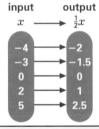

Comments

$x \rightarrow 0.5x$ or $\dfrac{x}{2}$ would be allowed.

Now try these!

1 For the function $x \rightarrow 2x - 3$ with input set $\{-1, 0, 1, 2, 3, 4\}$:

   a Draw a mapping diagram.

   b Draw and label a graph of the mapping.

2 a Draw a mapping diagram for the function shown on this graph.

   b Write down the equation of the mapping.

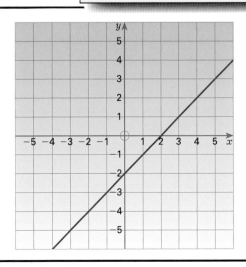

Straight-line graphs

 1 Lines on a grid that are horizontal have equations y = a number.

Lines on a grid that are vertical have equations x = a number.

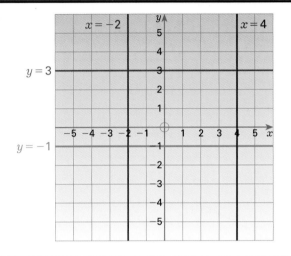

2 Most straight-line graphs have equations of the form $y = mx + c$.

m and c are fixed numbers that control how steep the graph is and where it crosses the y-axis.

m is called the **gradient** (steepness) of the graph.

c is called its y-**intercept**. For example:

equation	gradient (m)	y-intercept (c)
$y = 2x + 4$	2	4
$y = 2 - 3x$	-3	2
$y = x - 1$	1	-1
$y = 3$	0	3

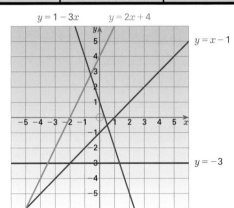

Lines with the same gradient are **parallel**.

 3 To find the equation of a line, find its gradient and intercept.

Look at this line:

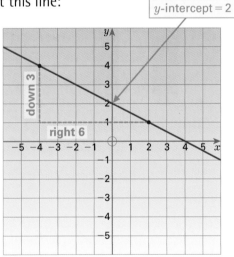

 y-intercept = 2

It crosses the y-axis at (0, 2) so its equation is $y = mx + 2$.

To find the gradient, take two points on the line and calculate

$$\text{gradient} = \frac{\text{increase in } y}{\text{increase in } x} = \frac{-3}{6} = -\frac{1}{2}.$$

So $y = -\frac{1}{2}x + 2$, or $y = 2 - \frac{1}{2}x$.

4 To plot a graph, simply calculate the coordinates of some points on it.

Two points are enough, but any two points can make a straight line, so plot a third point to check.

- **Horizontal and vertical lines have equations y = a number and x = a number.**
- **The gradient (m) and y-intercept (c) decide how steep the graph of $y = mx + c$ is, and exactly where it crosses the y-axis.**
- **Gradient is given by $\dfrac{\text{increase in } y}{\text{increase in } x}$ for any two points on the graph.**

Work-out!

Copy and complete

Complete the equation of a vertical line: _____ $= 5$

Complete the equation of a horizontal line: _____ $= -6$

The line with gradient 2 that crosses the y-axis at $(0, 5)$ has equation $y =$ ____ $x +$ ____

Parallel lines have the same _____ .

2 mins

Find the equation of the line that is parallel to $y = 2x$ and passes through the point (5, 3).

Questions and model answers

1 Find the point where the lines $y = 5 - x$ and $y = 3x + 1$ intersect. (1, 4)

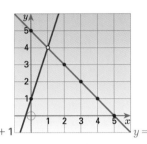

$y = 3x + 1$ $y = 5 - x$

Comments

The points on both lines with whole-number x-coordinates are shown on the graph.

Note that $x = 1$ is also the solution to the equation $5 - x = 3x + 1$.

2 Find the equation of the line given on this graph.

$y = -2x + 3$ or $y = 3 - 2x$

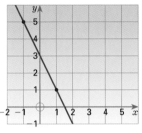

Comments

The graph crosses the y-axis at $(0, 3)$, so $c = 3$.

The gradient can be calculated from any two points on the graph, but the ones marked give

$$\text{gradient} = \frac{\text{increase in } y}{\text{increase in } x} = \frac{-4}{2} = -2, \text{ so } m = -2.$$

Level 7

3 Find the gradient of the line with equation:

$2x - 5y = 10.$ $2x - 5y = 10$

So $-2x + 5y = -10$ (swap all signs)

               $5y = -10 + 2x$ (add $2x$ to both sides)

               $y = -2 + \frac{2}{5}x$ (divide both sides by 5)

The gradient is $\frac{2}{5}$ or 0.4.

Comments

If the y-term is negative, It isn't necessary to change all the signs at the beginning, but be very careful and make sure it's done later on.

Now try these!

1a Draw a coordinate grid with x- and y-axes that range from -10 to 10.

b Plot the graph of $y = 4x - 5$.

c Plot the points $(-3, 9)$ and $(9, 5)$. Join them with a straight line. Find the equation of this line.

d What is the point of intersection of the two lines?

Level 7

On the grid used for the questions above, plot the graph of $4x + 3y = 1$.

What is its point of intersection with $y = 4x - 5$?

Multiples, factors and primes

 Multiples of a number are in its 'multiplication table'.

To generate multiples of a number, multiply it by 1, 2, 3, 4, 5, . . . in turn.

So the multiples of 7 begin: 7, 14, 21, 28, 35, etc.

 Factors of a number divide into it exactly, without leaving a remainder.

Factors always occur in pairs that multiply together to make the original number. For example, The factors of 24 are shown here:

Square numbers, such as 36, have one factor that pairs with itself:

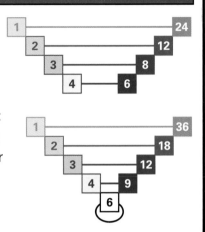

 Prime numbers have only two factors.

Their only multiples are 1 and themselves.

Numbers that are not prime are called **composite**.

 Common multiples are multiples of two or more numbers.

For example, the multiples of 8 are 8, 16, **24**, 32, 40, **48**, 56, 64, **72**, . . .

The multiples of 12 are 12, **24**, 36, **48**, 60, **72**, . . .

The **red** numbers (24, 48, 72, . . .) occur in both lists. They are the **common multiples of 8 and 12**. The lowest common multiple (LCM) is the smallest of them. Here, it's 24.

 Common factors are factors of two or more numbers.

Factors of 60: **1**, **2**, **3**, 4, **5**, **6**, **10**, 12, **15**, 20, **30**, 60.

Factors of 90: **1**, **2**, **3**, **5**, **6**, 9, **10**, **15**, 18, **30**, 45, 90.

The **blue** numbers (1, 2, 3, 5, 6, 10, 15, 30) occur in both lists and are the **common factors of 60 and 90**.

The highest common factor (HCF) is the largest of them. Here, it's 30.

 Any number can be written as the product of its prime factors.

For example, 2 and 3 are the prime factors of 6, and $6 = 2 \times 3$. The prime factors of 12 are also just 2 and 3, but you use 2 twice: $12 = 2 \times 2 \times 3$, or more neatly, $2^2 \times 3$.

To write a number using prime factors, break it into any two factors, then break these down, etc.

So $120 = 2 \times 2 \times 2 \times 3 \times 5$
$= 2^3 \times 3 \times 5.$

- **Multiples of a number are in its multiplication table. Common multiples are multiples of two or more numbers. The LCM is the lowest common multiple.**

- **Factors of a number divide into it exactly. Common factors are factors of two or more numbers. The HCF is the highest common factor.**

- **A prime number has only two factors: itself and 1. Any number can be written as a product of prime factors.**

Copy and complete

To calculate multiples of a number, multiply it by _____ , _____ , _____ , _____ , _____ , etc.

Factors of a number occur in _____ .

A prime number can only be divided exactly by _____ and _____ .

2 mins

In 1 minute, make a list of the denominators of fractions you know that don't make recurring decimals (for example, 4: $\frac{1}{4} = 0.25$, which doesn't recur). There are some ideas on pages 24–5 that might help you.

Is there a connection between these numbers? Hint: use prime factors!

Questions and model answers

1 Find all the factors of 40, and express 40 as a product of prime factors.

The factors of 40 are:
$\{1, 2, 4, 5, 8, 10, 20, 40\}$.
$40 = 2 \times 2 \times 2 \times 5$ or $2^3 \times 5$.

Comments

1 and 40 are factors. 40 is even, so 2 is and 20 must be factors. 4 is a factor, and so are 10 and 5, therefore 8 is too.

Once you have a factor list, spot the prime numbers (2 and 5) and use them to make 40.

2 What is the lowest common multiple of 12 and 14? 84

Multiples of 12:
12, 24, 36, 48, 60, 72, 84, 96, 108, . . .
Multiples of 14:
14, 28, 42, 56, 70, 84, 98, 112, . . .

Comments

You can also use prime factors. $12 = 2^2 \times 3$ and $14 = 2 \times 7$. To be a common multiple, when written using prime factors, a number must contain 2^2, 3 and 7. The smallest number that does this is $2^2 \times 3 \times 7 = 84$.

3 What is the highest common factor of 30, 48 and 56? 2

Factors of 30:
$\{1, 2, 3, 5, 6, 10, 15, 30\}$
Factors of 48:
$\{1, 2, 3, 4, 6, 8, 12, 16, 24, 48\}$
Factors of 56:
$\{1, 2, 4, 7, 8, 14, 28, 56\}$

Comments

You can also use prime factors. $30 = 2 \times 3 \times 5$, $48 = 2^4 \times 3$ and $56 = 2^3 \times 7$. To be a factor of all three, when written using prime factors, a number must contain only 2 (3 isn't a factor of 56, 5 isn't a factor of 48 or 56, 7 isn't a factor of 30 or 48).

Now try these!

1 Write down all the factors of each number. Express each one as a product of prime factors.

a 18	**b** 16	**c** 44	**d** 53
e 78	**f** 99	**g** 112	**h** 115

2 Find the LCM and HCF of:

a 12 and 16

b 35 and 45

c 8, 10 and 12

Number patterns and sequences

 1 A number pattern or sequence is a set of numbers that follows a rule.

For example, 1, 2, 1, 2, 1, 2 . . . is a repeating pattern. The three dots show that the pattern goes on forever.

The numbers in a sequence are called its **terms**.

Each term in a sequence has a **position**. The first term is in position 1, the second in position 2, etc.

 2 Linear sequences count up or down in fixed amounts.

To find the next term from the last one, always add or subtract the same number. This is the **term–to–term** rule for the sequence.

Examples: 5, 7, 9, 11, 13, . . . (term-to-term rule: *add 2*)

9, 5, 1, −3, −7, . . . (term-to-term rule: *subtract 4*)

2, 2.3, 2.6, 2.9, 3.2, . . . (term-to-term rule: *add 0.3*)

The same rule can give many different sequences, depending on what number you choose for the first term.

3 Different term-to-term rules make sequences that aren't linear.

Examples: 3, 6, 12, 24, 48, . . . (term-to-term rule: *multiply by 2*)

20, 2, 0.2, 0.02, 0.002, . . . (term-to-term rule: *divide by 10*)

8, 11, 17, 29, 53, . . . (term-to-term rule: *double and subtract 5*)

  5 There are some other sequences you should be familiar with.

Even numbers: 2, 4, 6, 8, 10, . . . (term-to-term rule: *add 2*)

Odd numbers: 1, 3, 5, 7, 9, . . . (term-to-term rule: *add 2*)

Cube numbers: 1, 8, 27, 64, 125, . . . (no simple term-to-term rule)

Powers of 2: 2, 4, 8, 16, 32, . . . (term-to-term rule: *multiply by 2*)

Powers of 10: 10, 100, 1000, . . . (term-to-term rule: *multiply by 10*)

Fibonacci sequence: 0, 1, 1, 2, 3, 5, 8, 13, . . . (add the last two terms to get the next one)

4 Some number patterns can be illustrated by patterns of dots.

Square numbers:

position				
1	**2**	**3**	**4**	**5**
1	4	9	16	25

add 3, 5, 7, 9, . . . to last term

Triangular numbers:

position				
1	**2**	**3**	**4**	**5**
1	3	6	10	15

add 2, 3, 4, 5, . . . to last term

 HELP! **Don't forget that sequences must follow a mathematical rule only. (Other kinds of rule are possible. For example, the numbers 3, 3, 5, 4, 4, 3, 5, 5, 4, 3, . . . are the number of letters in 'one, two, three, four, five, six, seven, eight, nine, ten'!)**

 Remember

- **Number patterns and sequences follow a mathematical rule.**

- **Sequences are made up of terms. Each term is in a particular position in the sequence.**

- **Linear sequences have term-to-term rules that involve adding or subtracting a fixed number.**

Copy and complete

In the sequence 4, 7, 10, 13, 16, 19, 22, . . .
The first _____ is 4. 13 is in the fourth _____ .
The _____ rule is 'add _____'.
This is a _____ sequence.

2 mins

Write down as many sequences as you can that begin 5, 10, . . . with their term-to-term rules.

Questions and model answers

1 The first term of a linear sequence is 3. The fifth term is 13.

a What is the term-to-term rule? Add 2.5

Whatever number is being added, to get from the first term to fifth, it has to be added four times. The difference between the first and fifth terms is 10. So the number added is
$10 \div 4 = 2.5$.

b Write down the first five terms.

3, 5.5, 8, 10.5, 13

c Find the tenth term. 25.5.

Add 2.5 to the fifth term 5 times to get the tenth term. $2.5 \times 5 = 12.5$ and $13 + 12.5 = 25.5$.

Comments

a You can only do this because the sequence is linear.

c To find the tenth term, you could just continue the sequence until it has 10 terms. The method here is much better if you want to find terms further along the sequence, such as the hundredth.

2 Use the term-to-term rule *divide by 2, then add 3* with first term 10, to make a sequence. Write down the first five terms. What happens if the sequence is continued for a large number of terms?

10, 8, 7, 6.5, 6.25

The terms gradually get closer and closer to 6.

Comments

Look at how far above 6 each term is: 4, 2, 1, 0.5, 0.25, . . . Each one is half the last, so they get smaller and smaller, approaching 0.

3 This table shows the triangular numbers, written 'out of step' in two columns.

Copy and complete the table, and comment on the result.

These are the square numbers.

triangular number	last triangular number	sum
1	-	1 + 0 = 1
3	1	3 + 1 = 4
6	3	9
10	6	16
15	10	25
21	15	36
28	21	49

Comments

A dot diagram illustrates this well.

Now try these!

1 Continue each of the following patterns until it has eight terms.

a 2, 5, 8, 11, 14, . . .

b 29, 24, 19, 14, 9, . . .

c 1.3, 1.55, 1.8, 2.05, 2.3, . . .

d 10, 12, 16, 22, 30, . . .

e 7, 14, 28, 56, 112, . . .

f 1, 8, 27, 64, 125, . . .

2 A linear sequence has first term 8 and third term 20. What is the term-to-term rule, and what is the fifth term?

3 Using the term-to-term rule: *add 10, then divide by 10* and first term 9, write down the first five terms of the sequence. What happens if the sequence is continued for a large number of terms?

Sequences and formulae

1 *Most sequences have a position-to-term rule.*

This means that you calculate the term in a sequence from its position, not from the last term.

Position-to-term rules can be written down as formulae. In this book, T is used for the terms and n for the positions. The sequence is made by substituting (see pages 32–3) $n = 1, 2, 3, 4, 5, \ldots$ into the formula.

T is sometimes called the nth term of the sequence.

Example: the formula $T = n + 3$ gives the sequence 4, 5, 6, 7, 8, ... This is because when $n = 1$, $T = 1 + 3 = 4$. When $n = 2$, $T = 2 + 3 = 5$, and so on.

3 *Linear sequences that decrease have a negative number of n in their formulae.*

The formula must contain $T = -3n$ to decrease at the right rate. However, 12 needs to be added to every term to match the

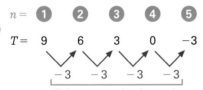

This means the formula contains $T = -3n$

numbers in the sequence. So the formula is $T = -3n + 12$, or, more neatly $T = 12 - 3n$.

Level 7

Quadratic sequences contain n^2 in their formulae. To find the number of n^2s, continue the difference table down to a second difference row. If the number is constant (e.g. 6), halve it to get the number of n^2s (e.g. $3n^2$).

See the model answer on p. 50 for more detail.

Don't get term-to-term and position-to-term rules mixed up. If that happens, you're likely to think that the formula for the sequence in the second box is $T = n + 4$.

HELP!

2 *To find the formula for a linear sequence, use a difference table.*

Example:

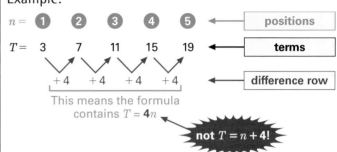

This means the formula contains $T = 4n$

not $T = n + 4$!

The terms of the sequence increase four times as fast as the position numbers, so the rule must contain $T = 4n$ to make this happen. That isn't enough, though, or the sequence would be 4, 8, 12, 16, 20, . . . These terms are all 1 less than that, so the formula is $T = 4n - 1$.

Always check your formula by substituting values and calculating the terms. If they don't match the original sequence, you've made a mistake.

4 *Some sequences that are not linear still have simple formulae.*

Even numbers:	2, 4, 6, 8, 10, . . .	$T = 2n$
Odd numbers:	1, 3, 5, 7, 9, . . .	$T = 2n - 1$
Square numbers:	1, 4, 9, 16, 25, . . .	$T = n^2$
Cube numbers:	1, 8, 27, 64, 125, . . .	$T = n^3$
Powers of 2:	2, 4, 8, 16, 32, . . .	$T = 2^n$
Powers of 10:	10, 100, 1000, 10 000, . . .	$T = 10^n$

Remember

- The position-to-term rule for a linear sequence can be found using a difference table.

- Given a formula, substitute position numbers into it to find the corresponding terms.

- Quadratic sequences can be analysed using a second difference row.

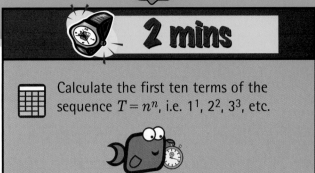

Work-out!

2 mins

Calculate the first ten terms of the sequence $T = n^n$, i.e. 1^1, 2^2, 3^3, etc.

Copy and complete

You can use a formula to calculate the _____ in a sequence from their _____ .

Use a _____ _____ to analyse linear sequences.

Questions and model answers

Level 7

1 Generate the first five terms of the sequences with the following formulae.

a $T = 5n + 1$ 6, 11, 16, 21, 26, . . .
b $T = 8 - n$ 7, 6, 5, 4, 3, . . .
c $T = 2.5n - 1.5$ 1, 3.5, 6, 8.5, 11, . . .
d $T = n^2 + 4n - 4$ 1, 8, 17, 28, 41, . . .
e $T = 3^n$ 3, 9, 27, 81, 243, . . .

2 a Find the formula for the sequence that begins 3, 10, 17, 24, 31, . . .

$T = 7n - 4$

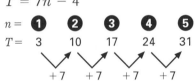

n = ① ② ③ ④ ⑤
T = 3 10 17 24 31
  +7 +7 +7 +7

b Calculate the 50th term of the sequence.

$7 \times 50 - 4 = 350 - 4 = 346$

c Is 100 a term of the sequence? If not, which two terms does it fall between?

No. It falls between the 14th and 15th terms (94 and 101).

3 Find the formula for the sequence that begins 1, 7, 21, 43, 73 . . .

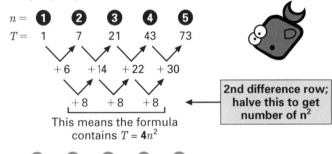

n = ① ② ③ ④ ⑤
T = 1 7 21 43 73
    +6 +14 +22 +30
      +8 +8 +8

2nd difference row; halve this to get number of n^2

This means the formula contains $T = 4n^2$

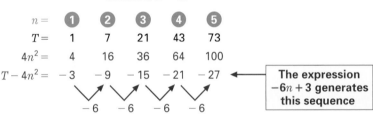

n = ① ② ③ ④ ⑤
T = 1 7 21 43 73
$4n^2 =$ 4 16 36 64 100
$T - 4n^2 =$ −3 −9 −15 −21 −27
    −6 −6 −6 −6

The expression $-6n + 3$ generates this sequence

Combining the results from both parts, $T = 4n^2 - 6n + 3$.

Comments

2 If 100 is a term, then there's a whole number n such that $7n - 4 = 100$. Solving this equation gives $n = 14.857 . . .$, so 100 is between the 14th and 15th terms.

3 The differences are all 7, so the formula contains $T = 7n$. $T = 7n$ would generate the terms 7, 14, 21, . . .: the terms in this sequence are 4 less than those.

Now try these!

1 Generate the first five terms of the sequences with the following formulae.

a $T = 4n + 2$ b $T = 4 - 3n$
c $T = 5n - 5$ d $T = 2n^2 + 1$

① ② ③ ④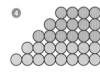

2 These patterns are made up of green balls and pink balls.

a Find formulae for the number of each colour of ball in the nth pattern.

Metric and imperial units

1 There are units in the metric system for many different quantities.

quantity	unit	abbreviation
length/distance	metre	m
mass	gram	g
time	second	s
area	square metre	m²
volume	cubic metre	m³
capacity	litre	l

2 By adding prefixes to the basic units, you can make different sizes of unit for different purposes. These are the most commonly used ones.

scale factor	prefix	abbreviation	example
× 1000	kilo-	k	kilometre (km)
÷ 100	centi-	c	centilitre (cl)
÷ 1000	milli-	m	milligram (mg)
÷ 1 000 000	micro-	μ	microsecond (μs)

Also: 1000 kg = 1 tonne (t) and 10 000 m² = 1 hectare (ha).

Notice that mega- (M) = × 1 million and giga- (G) = × 1 billion are also used, mostly in computing. They are hardly ever used with the units above.

3 To convert a quantity from one metric unit to another, follow these steps.

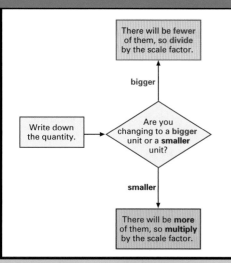

- There will be **fewer** of them, so **divide** by the scale factor.
- **bigger**
- Write down the quantity.
- Are you changing to a **bigger** unit or a **smaller** unit?
- **smaller**
- There will be **more** of them, so **multiply** by the scale factor.

4 Imperial units are older units that are still in common use.

The most important conversions are shown in red.

1 inch (in) = 2.5 cm	1 foot (ft) = 12 in = 30 cm
1 yard (yd) = 3 ft = 0.92 m	1 mile (mi or m) = 1760 yd = 1.6 km
1 ounce (oz) = 28 g	1 pound (lb) = 16 oz = 0.45 kg
1 stone (st) = 14 lb = 6.4 kg	1 ton ≈ 1 tonne
1 pint (pt) = 57 cl or 0.57 l	1 gallon (gal) = 8 pt = 4.5 l

When giving answers:
- use a sensible size of unit
- round to a sensible accuracy.

This helps you avoid statements like 'The distance from London to Birmingham is 11 735 686 cm'. It might be true, but it's not very useful!

Level 7

When a measurement is given correct to the nearest unit, it can be out by up to half a unit either way. For example, if your height (H) is 162 cm correct to the nearest cm then, in reality, $161.5 \text{ cm} \leq H < 162.5 \text{ cm}$. Note that 162.5 itself isn't allowed, because that would round up to 163.

Remember

- Metric units are based on a system of tens, like our number system. This makes them easy to calculate with.
- Imperial units are still in use, particularly on road signs. It is useful to memorise the most common conversions.

Copy and complete

1 kilogram = _____ grams

1 millimetre = _____ centimetres

6 feet = _____ inches = _____ cm

 2 mins

For the imperial units in section 4, work out the inverse conversions, such as 1 kg = 2.2 lb.

Questions and model answers

1 What mass is shown on this scale?

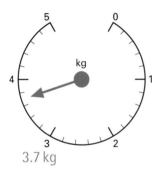

3.7 kg

Comments

The scale has five divisions per kg, so each division is 0.2 kg.

2 Masoud is 5 feet 4 inches tall. What is his height in metres?

5 ft = 5 × 12 = 60 in, so Masoud is 64 in tall.

64 × 2.5 = 160 cm = 1.6 m.

Comments

You could also use 1 ft = 30 cm and calculate 5 × 30 + 4 × 2.5 = 150 + 10 = 160 cm.

3 Jeannette needs a litre of orange juice. She only has cartons containing 180 ml each. How many does she need to open?

1000 ÷ 180 = 5.5̇, so she needs six cartons.

Comments

You could also work in litres. 1 ÷ 0.18 gives the same answer.

Level 7

4 A rectangle is 6 cm long and 4 cm wide. The measurements are given to the nearest centimetre. What is the maximum possible perimeter of the rectangle?

The length can be anything up to 6.5 cm, and the width 4.5 cm.

So the perimeter can be anything up to 6.5 × 2 + 4.5 × 2 = 13 + 9 = 22 cm.

Comments

Note that 22 cm itself is not a possible value: the perimeter must be less than this.

Now try these!

1 Copy and complete the table. Each row represents one quantity.

20 kg	_____ t	_____ g
_____ m	1.55 km	_____ mm
285 ml	_____ cl	_____ l

2 Maxine weighs 7 st 9 lb. What is her weight in kg?

3 A 50 p piece weighs 15 g.

   a At a bank, £10 worth of 50 pence pieces are kept in a bag. What do this many 50 pence pieces weigh?

   b How many 50 pence pieces would you need to balance a kilogram of sugar?

4 A bus travels the following distances between stops: 230 m, 520 m, 1.3 km, 2.45 km, 480 m, 150 m. How long is its route? Give your answer in kilometres.

Level 7

Calculate the lowest and highest possible areas for the 6 cm by 4 cm rectangle in model answer 4 above.

Time calculations

1 Units of time are not linked by factors of 10.

There are 60 seconds in a minute, 60 minutes in an hour and 24 hours in a day.
So, to convert a time in minutes to seconds, multiply by 60, etc.

2 There are two ways of writing the time of day: the 12-hour clock and the 24-hour clock.

12-hour	1 am	2 am	3 am	4 am	5 am	6 am	7 am	8 am	9 am	10 am	11 am	12 noon
24-hour	0100	0200	0300	0400	0500	0600	0700	0800	0900	1000	1100	1200

12-hour	1 pm	2 pm	3 pm	4 pm	5 pm	6 pm	7 pm	8 pm	9 pm	10 pm	11 pm	12 midnight
24-hour	1300	1400	1500	1600	1700	1800	1900	2000	2100	2200	2300	2400

3 You can tackle time calculations in two ways.

For Paper 1, addition and subtraction is best done in columns. Remember that you borrow or carry 60 units. Alternatively, if you want to calculate the difference between two times, you can count on to the next minute/hour, etc. (see model answer 1 on page 56 for an example).

For Paper 2, work in the smallest unit involved. Convert times in hours and minutes to minutes only. Convert times in minutes and seconds or hours, minutes and seconds to seconds only. You may need to jot down these figures and/or store them in your calculator's memory.

4 For Paper 1, to multiply a time by a number, work in separate columns. For instance, to multiply 5 minutes 36 seconds by 8:

$$
\begin{array}{r r}
\text{min} & \text{sec} \\
5 & 36 \\
\times & 8 \\
\hline
40 & 288 \\
\end{array}
$$

240 sec = 4 min, so
288 sec = 4 min 48 sec

$$
\begin{array}{r r}
\text{min} & \text{sec} \\
40 & \\
+ \quad 4 & 48 \\
\hline
44 & 48 \\
\end{array}
$$

When dividing, the only safe way to do it is to work in the smallest unit.

Reverse the multiplication and divide 44 min 48 s by 8, convert 44 min 48 s:
$(44 \times 60 + 48) = 2688$ s

Then divide by 8 to get
336 s = 5 min 36 s.

Remember

- **Time units aren't related in tens, but in sixties.**
- **When using a calculator for work on time, convert to the smallest possible unit before calculating.**

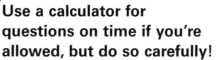  HELP!

Use a calculator for questions on time if you're allowed, but do so carefully!
If you try the multiplication example from section 4 by typing 5.36×8, you'll get 42.88, 42 minutes and 88 seconds! This is obviously wrong, because the number of 'seconds' is over 60, but there are times when the answer looks reasonable, so be careful!

Copy and complete

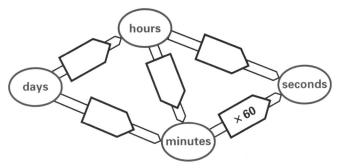

This conversion chart shows what you must multiply by to change from one time unit to another. For example, it shows that to convert a time interval from minutes to seconds, you multiply by 60.

2 mins

How many seconds are there in a year?

Questions and model answers

1 A video timer switched itself on at 02:35:41 and off again at 04:18:20. How long did it record for?   1 hour 42 min 39 s

Comments

Two methods are available.

Subtract in columns:

$$\begin{array}{r} \overset{77}{\cancel{04}} : \overset{17}{\cancel{18}} : \overset{80}{\cancel{20}} \\ - 02 : 35 : 41 \\ \hline 1 : 42 : 39 \end{array}$$

Count on:
```
                    1 hour
          24 + 18 = 42 min
          19 + 20 = 39 sec
          Answer: 1 hour 42 min 39 sec
```

02:35:41 02:36:00 03:00:00 04:00:00 04:18:00 04:18:20

    19 sec   24 min   1 hour   18 min   20 sec

2 A radio drama, lasting 2 hours 50 minutes, is to be broadcast as eight episodes of equal length. How long is each episode?

2 h 50 min = 2 × 3600 + 50 × 60 = 10 200 s;
10 200 ÷ 8 = 1275 s = 21 min 15 s

Comments

If you convert to minutes, rather than seconds, for this calculation, you get:
2 hours 50 minutes = 2 × 60 + 50 = 170 min. 170 ÷ 8 = 21.25 min. If you're happy that 0.25 minutes = 15 seconds, that's OK. Otherwise, work in seconds!

Now try these!

1 Alicia records two films. The first is 1 hour 56 minutes long. The second is 2 hours 16 minutes long. When the video starts recording, the counter reads 2:35:44. What does it read at the end of the recording?

2 What is the total length of 12 boxing rounds of 3 min 30 s each?

Time-based graphs

1 *Some graphs plot a quantity (usually on the y-axis) against time (usually on the x-axis). A patient's temperature graph in hospital is a time-based graph.*

This graph shows the output of a power station over one day:

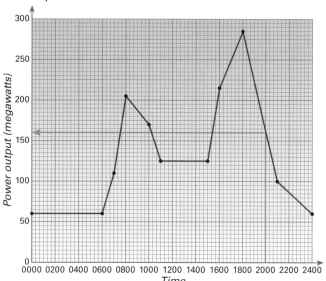

The green arrow shows the graph being used to estimate the power at 2000 (about 160 MW).

Steeper lines show where the output is increasing or decreasing faster.

Horizontal lines show where the output is constant (not changing).

Don't fall into the trap of interpreting graphs in a non-mathematical way. How's this as a description of the journey in the second section?

'I climbed up the hill for an hour, then walked along a flat bit. I finished climbing two hours after I started. I crossed the top in an hour, then went straight down the other side, apart from walking along a short ledge.'

It's rubbish, of course! Read the descriptions on the axes carefully.

2 *Graphs where distance is plotted against time are sometimes called travel graphs.*

This graph shows a sponsored walk:

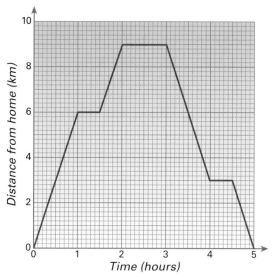

A description of the walk could be, 'I walked at a steady speed for an hour, then stopped for half an hour. I walked for another half hour, then stopped for lunch (1 hour). I walked back at a steady speed, with a half-hour break'.

Note that there are 10 divisions to an hour on the time axis. This means that each division represents $\frac{1}{10}$ of an hour, or 6 minutes. The short stop on the return journey is therefore 12 minutes long.

On a graph of this type, a **horizontal** line means the object or person is **stationary** (not moving). Any other **straight** line shows movement at a **steady speed**. The **gradient** (see page 40) of the line represents the speed.

- **On any time-based graph, check the divisions on the time axis carefully.**
- **On a travel graph, a horizontal line indicates no motion.**
- **The steepness of a travel graph represents the speed of the moving object.**

Copy and complete

On graph paper, draw and label a set of axes for a graph of a 240 km train journey, lasting $1\frac{1}{2}$ hours (you will need this later).

2 mins

Using the axes you drew in *Copy and complete* earlier, draw a straight line to represent the journey. After one hour, how far had the train travelled?

Question and model answer

1 This graph shows the temperature of the water in a domestic hot-water tank. Use it to answer the questions.

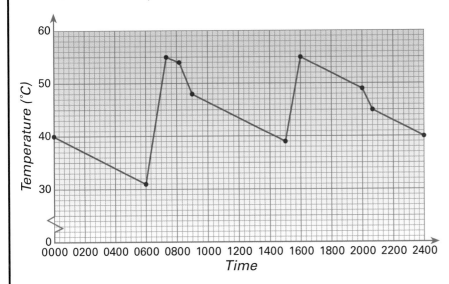

a What was the water temperature at 10 pm? 43 °C

b At what times was the temperature 35 °C? 0320 and 0615

c The water heater switched on at 6 am. When did it turn off again? 7.30 am

d What was the rise in temperature when the water heater switched on in the afternoon? 16 °C

e For how long was the water heater switched off during the morning and afternoon? $7\frac{1}{2}$ hours

Now try this!

a On graph paper, draw axes with time running from 1000–1500 (2 cm to 1 hour) and distance from Wilston running from 0–50 miles (2 cm to 10 miles).

b Plot the following journey on your graph:

The coach left Wilston at 1000. We arrived at Conisham, 25 miles away, after $\frac{3}{4}$ hour, where we stopped for 15 minutes. We then drove on to Fortley Castle, a further 17 miles, arriving at 1130. We stayed there for an hour and three-quarters, then set off back to Wilston, arriving at 1445. We made a short stop at a service area 10 km from Wilston. We stopped there for 9 minutes, and it took us half an hour to get home after that.

Angle facts

1 Where lines join, or intersect, they form angles.

The angle between two lines is the number of degrees you have to turn one so it is on top of the other. The lines making an angle are called its **arms** – their length is irrelevant. The point where the arms meet or cross is the **vertex** of the angle. Different amounts of turning have different names.

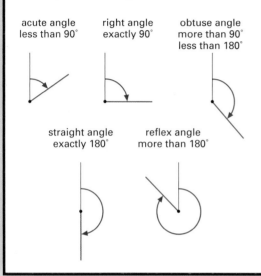

acute angle
less than 90°

right angle
exactly 90°

obtuse angle
more than 90°
less than 180°

straight angle
exactly 180°

reflex angle
more than 180°

2 Intersecting lines form related angles.

Adjacent angles on a
straight line add up to 180°

$x + y = 180°$

Angles at a point
add up to 360°

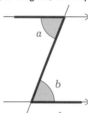

$a + b + c + d = 360°$

Vertically opposite
angles are equal

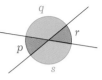

$p = r$ and $q = s$

3 When a transversal line cuts across parallel lines, related angles are formed.

Parallel lines are indicated by arrows.

Alternate angles
('**Z**' angles) are equal

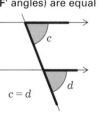

$a = b$

Corresponding angles
('**F**' angles) are equal

$c = d$

Allied angles ('**C**' angles)
add up to 180°

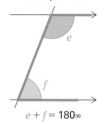

$e + f = 180°$

Remember '**Z**', '**F**' and '**C**'.

4 The angle sum of a triangle is 180°.

This is true for every triangle, whatever type it is. The interior angles always total 180°. So if you know two angles in a triangle, it's easy to calculate the third.

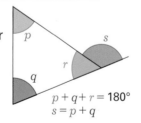

$p + q + r = 180°$
$s = p + q$

This means that the sum of any two angles in the triangle is equal to the opposite **exterior** angle.

5 The angle sum of a quadrilateral is 360°.

This is true for every quadrilateral, whatever type it is — even if it contains a reflex angle!

HELP!

If you have trouble remembering which types of angle are equal and which add up to a total, imagine what would happen if you rotated one of the lines. Do the angles stay the same as each other, or is their total constant?

Remember

- **When lines join or intersect, angles are formed.**

- **Various types of angles are equal to each other, add up to 180° or add up to 360°.**

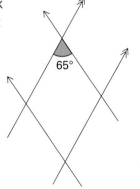
Copy and complete

Write angle facts in the correct boxes.

... are equal | ... add up to 180° | ... add up to 360°

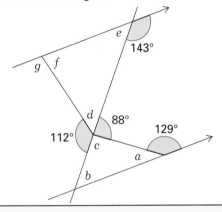

2 mins

Draw a large triangle. Mark a point near the centre. Joint the point to all three vertices with straight lines. This creates three triangles. Measure and label all the angles. Check that the angles in all three triangles total 180°, and that the angles at the central point total 360°.

Questions and model answers

1 Label all the angles in this diagram with their sizes in degrees.

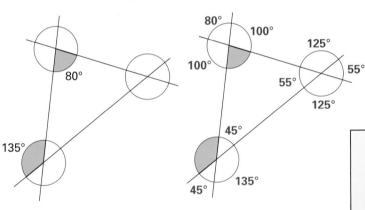

80°
80°
135°

80° 100°
100° 125°
55° 55°
125°
45°
45° 135°

2 Find the angles marked with letters.

e
143°
g f
d 88°
112° c 129°
b a

Comments

The angles around each vertex are found using adjacent angles on a straight line and vertically opposite angles. The 55° angle is found using the angle sum of the triangle.

Answers and comments

$a = 51°$ (adjacent to 129°)
$b = 37°$ (allied with 143°)
$c = 92°$ (angle sum of triangle)
$d = 68°$ (angles at a point, or adjacent to 112°)
$e = 37°$ (alternate with b, or adjacent to 143°)
$f = 75°$ (angle sum of triangle)
$g = 105°$ (adjacent to f)

Now try these!

1 Find the angles labelled with letters.

2 I want to draw a quadrilateral with angles of 40°, 60°, 120° and 150°. Is this possible?

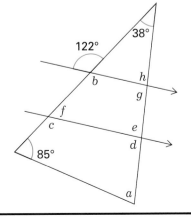

38°
122°
b h
g
f
c e
d
85°
a

3 Copy the diagram. Mark on it all the angles that are equal to 65°.

65°

Symmetry:
rotations and reflections: congruence

 1 Reflection produces a 'mirror image' of a shape or pattern.

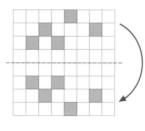

Reflection is an example of a **transformation** of a shape. The starting shape is called the **object** of the transformation. The resulting shape is called the **image**.

Matching points of the object and its reflection are equal distances from the mirror line.

To describe a reflection you need the equation of the mirror line.

 2 A shape or pattern that looks the same when reflected has line symmetry.

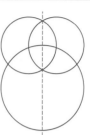

There may be more than one line of symmetry (mirror line).

Line symmetry is also known as **reflective symmetry** or **bilateral symmetry**.

 3 When a shape is turned through an angle around a fixed point, it has been rotated.

The fixed point is called the **centre of rotation**. In this diagram, the rotation is 90° anticlockwise.

 centre

Rotation is another type of transformation. To find the centre of rotation, use a piece of tracing paper and try out different centres, until the image is in the right place.

To describe a rotation you need the centre, angle and direction.

HELP!

 4 A shape or pattern that looks the same when rotated has rotational symmetry.

The **order of rotational symmetry** is the number of positions, during a full turn, where the shape looks the same. The angle between positions is always $\frac{360°}{\text{order}}$.

order 4   order 2   order 6

Mathematical 'mirrors' are double-sided! That means that if the mirror line goes through the object, parts of the image will appear on both sides of it. So don't forget to reflect parts of the object on both sides of the mirror line.

 5 Two shapes that are identical are said to be congruent.

It doesn't matter if one is reflected or rotated.

original shape	These are congruent to the original shape.	These are similar to the original shape (see page 72).	These look a bit like the original shape but are different.

 Remember

- **Reflections and rotations take an object shape and produce an image shape.**

- **A shape or pattern can have two types of symmetry: line symmetry or rotational symmetry.**

Work-out!

Copy and complete

Write down the information needed to describe completely:

a a reflection

b a rotation.

2 mins

On squared paper, try out the effect of using different centres of rotation on a simple shape, keeping the angle of rotation the same.

Questions and model answers

1 Reflect the patterns of squares using the given mirror lines.

 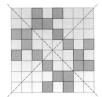

Comments

Using the 'diagonal' mirrors on the second grid is quite difficult: turn the paper round so the lines look horizontal and vertical. Covering up any parts of the diagram you're not using is also quite helpful.

2 a Describe completely the transformation with image shape P and object shape Q.

Reflection in the line $y = 1$ (see page 40 for more information on straight-line graphs).

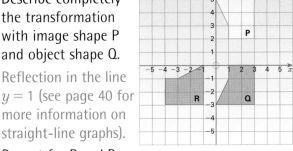

b Repeat for P and R.

Rotation, 90° clockwise about centre (−3, 3).

Comments

You may not be asked for the equation of the mirror line. You may only have to mark it on a diagram.

Now try these!

1

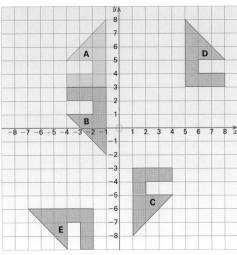

a Describe completely the transformation with image shape A and object shape B.

b Repeat for A → C, A → D and A → E.

2 Copy the grids below. Reflect the line patterns of squares using the given mirror lines.

3 For each shape, write down the number of lines of symmetry it has, and its order of rotational symmetry.

a b c

Triangles and quadrilaterals

1
Special types of triangle have particular names.

Tick marks are used to show sides of equal length. Angles that are coloured the same are the same size.

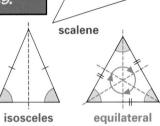

scalene

isosceles

equilateral

	isosceles triangle	equilateral triangle
equal sides	2	3
equal angles	2	3
lines of symmetry	1	3
order of rotational symmetry	1	3

2
There are several special types of quadrilateral.

general quadrilateral (no special features) kite trapezium isosceles trapezium parallelogram rhombus rectangle square

	kite	trapezium	isosceles trapezium	parallelogram	rhombus	rectangle	square
equal sides	2 pairs		2	2 pairs	4	2 pairs	4
parallel sides		1 pair	1 pair	2 pairs	2 pairs	2 pairs	2 pairs
equal angles	2		2 pairs	2 pairs	2 pairs	4	4
lines of symmetry	1		1		2	2	4
order of rotational symmetry	1	1	1	2	2	2	4
diagonals bisect each other?				yes	yes	yes	yes
diagonals perpendicular?	yes				yes		yes

3
Follow these rules to construct a triangle accurately.

- You will always have **at least one** side given. Pick one and draw it.
- When adding an angle to your drawing, make the new 'arm' of the angle as long as possible. It should eventually intersect another feature of your drawing to give the third vertex.
- When adding a side with a known length, set your compass to the length of the side. Put the compass point on the vertex, then trace out an arc. This arc should intersect another feature of your drawing to give the third vertex.

You may be given a sketch diagram to help you.

HELP!

Some types of quadrilateral are special versions of another type. For example, a square is a special type of rectangle with all sides the same.

Remember

- Special types of triangles and quadrilaterals have properties that allow you to find unknown sides and angles.
- To construct a triangle accurately, start with a given side, then add the other sides/angles until the position of the third vertex is obvious.

Copy and complete

A triangle with no lines of symmetry is

_____ .

A quadrilateral with just two lines of symmetry could be a _____ or a

_____ .

Mark the equal angles/sides and parallel sides on a sketch of a parallelogram.

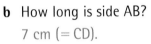 **2 mins**

Usually, any diagonal of a quadrilateral will split it into two triangles. Use the diagrams on page 61 to answer these questions for each type of quadrilateral:

a are the triangles of any special type?

b are the triangles congruent, similar or totally different?

Questions and model answers

1 Find the angles marked with letters in the triangles.

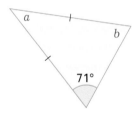

The triangle is isosceles, so $b = 71°$.
From the angle sum of the triangle,
$a = 180° - 2 \times 71° = 180° - 142° = 38°$.

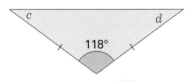

The triangle is isosceles, so $c = d$.
From the angle sum of the triangle,
$c + d = 180° - 118° = 62°$. So, $c = d = 31°$.

2 Here is a sketch of a quadrilateral:

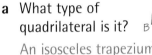

a What type of quadrilateral is it?

An isosceles trapezium.

b How long is side AB?

7 cm (= CD).

c What is angle D?

99° (allied with C or = A by symmetry).

d Is it possible to say how long side BC is?

Not without further work.

Comments

a It's a trapezium because angles A and B add up to 180°, meaning AD is parallel to BC. It's isosceles because angles B and C are equal.

b The length of BC can be found by measuring an accurate drawing (18.2 cm to 1 d.p.).

Now try these!

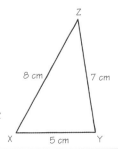

1 Copy this sketch diagram of a kite. Correctly label as many angles and sides as you can.

2 Draw this triangle accurately. Measure angles X, Y and Z.

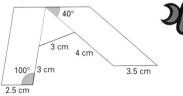

3 This octagon is a compound of two parallelograms and an equilateral triangle.

There's enough information in the diagram to work out all the other sides and angles.

Copy the diagram and label them in the correct places.

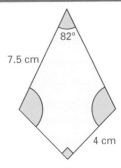

Polygons

1 Polygons are connected shapes with three or more straight sides.

Regular polygons have all sides equal and all angles equal.

In all formulae on this page, n will be used for 'the number of sides'.

number of sides (n)	3	4	5	6	7	8	9	10	12
name	triangle	quadrilateral	pentagon	hexagon	heptagon	octagon	nonagon	decagon	dodecagon

2 The *exterior* angles of any polygon total 360°.

So, in a regular polygon, the size of one exterior angle is $e = \dfrac{360°}{n}$.
This means that one interior angle $i = 180° - e = 180° - \dfrac{360°}{n}$.

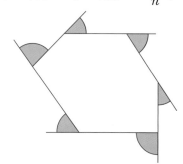

3 The angle sum of a polygon is related to the number of triangles you can split it into.

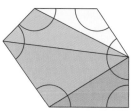

Each angle of the polygon forms part of an angle in one of the triangles. Nothing is added or missed out. So the interior angles in this hexagon add up to $4 \times 180° = 720°$.

number of sides (n)	number of triangles	angle sum (S)	interior angle in regular polygon (i)
3	1	$1 \times 180° = 180°$	$180° \div 3 = 60°$
4	2	$2 \times 180° = 360°$	$360° \div 4 = 90°$
5	3	$3 \times 180° = 540°$	$540° \div 5 = 108°$
6	4	$4 \times 180° = 720°$	$720° \div 6 = 120°$

The number of triangles is always **two less** than the number of sides, $(n - 2)$.
So $S = 180(n - 2)°$ or $(180n - 360)°$.
In a **regular** polygon, divide the angle sum by the number of sides to find the size of one interior angle; $i = \dfrac{S}{n}$.

4 It's possible to find the number of sides of a polygon if you know something about the angles.

If you know the angle sum, do this:

angle sum (S) → **÷ 180** → number of triangles → **+ 2** → number of sides (n)

To calculate the number of sides of a regular polygon if you know the interior angle, find the exterior angle first.

interior angle (i) → **subtract this from 180** → exterior angle (e) → **divide 360 by this** → number of sides (n)

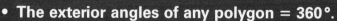

- **The exterior angles of any polygon = 360°.**
- **The angle sum of a polygon depends on the number of triangles it can be split into.**
- **Regular polygons have all angles equal and all sides equal.**

Copy and complete

number of sides (n)		5	6	8	10	12
name		pentagon				
angle sum (S)		$3 \times 180° = 540°$				
interior angle in regular polygon (i)		$540° \div 5 = 108°$				
exterior angle in regular polygon (e)		$360° \div 5 = 72°$				
check ($i + e$)		$108° + 72° = 180°$ ✓				

2 mins

Work out whether the following angles could be the exterior angles of a regular polygon.

a 15° **b** 30°

c 150° **d** 45°

e 50° **f** 120°

g 135° **h** 6°

Questions and model answers

1 a What is the angle sum of an icosagon (20 sides)?

An icosagon splits into $20 - 2 = 18$ triangles. These total $18 \times 180° = 3240°$.

b What is the size of one interior angle of a regular icosagon? $3240° \div 20 = 162°$

c What is the size of one exterior angle?

$180° - 162° = 18°$

2 The diagram shows part of a regular polygon.

How many sides does it have?

The interior angles are all 156°. That means

the exterior angles are all $180° - 156° = 24°$. $360° \div 24° = 15$. The polygon has 15 sides.

Comments

Note that you can't find the number of sides by finding the angle sum and then the 'number of triangles', as you would need to know the answer already!

Comments

You could have found the answer to part (c) by calculating $360° \div 20 = 18°$.

Now try these!

1 Find the unmarked angle in this pentagon.

2 a What is the angle sum of a polygon with 24 sides?

b What is the size of one interior angle of a regular 24-sided polygon?

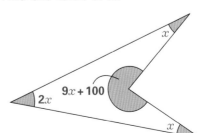

c What is the size of one exterior angle?

3 A regular polygon has interior angles of 140°. How many sides does it have?

4 Find the value of x.

Area: rectangles and compound and shapes

1 To calculate the area of a rectangle, multiply width by height.

In algebra, this can be written $A = lw$.

length (l)

width (w)

2 If you know the area of a rectangle and one of the sides, you can work out the other side.

Just divide the area by the known side.

In algebra, make w or l the subject of the area formula: $w = \dfrac{A}{l}$ or $l = \dfrac{A}{w}$.

3 Squares are rectangles too, but have their own formulae.

To find the area of a square, square one of the sides: $A = s \times s = s^2$.

To find the side length if you know the area, square root it: $s = \sqrt{A}$.

side (s)

side (s)

HELP!

When calculating an area, check that the sides you're multiplying are in the same units. It's no good multiplying 2 m by 40 cm to get 80, for example. You need to multiply 200 cm by 40 cm to get 8000 cm², or 2 m × 0.4 m = 0.8 m². As there are 10 000 cm² in 1 m², these answers are the same.

4 Compound shapes are formed from more than one rectangle.

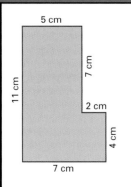

5 cm

7 cm

11 cm

2 cm

4 cm

7 cm

They can be made by putting rectangles together, or cutting out one rectangle from another. To calculate the area of a compound shape, split it into rectangular parts. There may be several ways to do this.

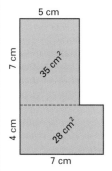

5 cm

7 cm

35 cm²

4 cm

28 cm²

7 cm

$5 \times 7 = 35$ cm²
$7 \times 4 = 28$ cm²
$35 + 28 = 63$ cm²

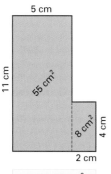

5 cm

11 cm

55 cm²

8 cm²

4 cm

2 cm

$5 \times 11 = 55$ cm²
$2 \times 4 = 8$ cm²
$55 + 8 = 63$ cm²

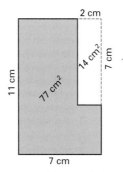

2 cm

11 cm

77 cm²

14 cm²

7 cm

4 cm

7 cm

$7 \times 11 = 77$ cm²
$2 \times 7 = 14$ cm²
$77 - 14 = 63$ cm²

Remember

- To find the area of a rectangle, multiply length by width.

- Square the side of a square to get its area.

- Split compound shapes into a number of rectangles.

Copy and complete

This rectangle has perimeter 20 cm.

9 cm

1 cm

Copy it, then sketch as many other rectangles as you can with perimeter 20 cm. Calculate their areas. Which one has the largest area?

2 mins

All the rectangles in this table have area 10 cm². Copy and complete the table, rounding answers to 1 d.p. where necessary.

width	0.5 cm	1 cm	2 cm	3 cm	4 cm	5 cm
length						

width	6 cm	7 cm	8 cm	9 cm	10 cm	15 cm
length						

Questions and model answers

1 **a** Calculate the area of this rectangle.

32 cm

0.8 mm

$32 \times 0.08 = 2.56 \ cm^2$

b How large is a square with the same area as the rectangle?

side $= \sqrt{2.56} = 1.6$ cm

Comments

a Either width has to be changed to 0.08 cm, or length to 320 mm.

2 Find the area of this shape.

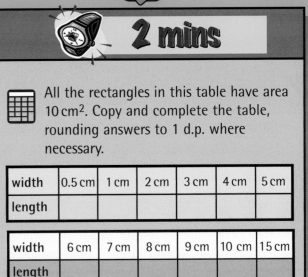

Comments

There are many ways to split the shape up.
Here is one:

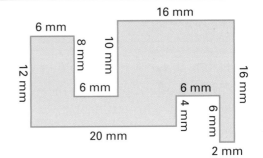

3 A satellite photograph of the Earth covers a rectangular area of 300 km². The rectangle is 24 km long. How wide is it? $300 \div 24 = 12.5$ km

Now try these!

1 Each row in the table represents one rectangle. Copy and complete it.

length	width	area
21 cm	35 cm	
8 m	8 m	
	4.5 m	81 m²
12.5 cm		400 mm²
	1.6 km	20 km²

2 Calculate the area of this shape.

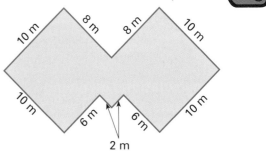

Area: triangles, parallelograms and trapezia

 1 The *perpendicular height* is an important measurement common to triangles, parallelograms and trapezia.

The perpendicular height is shown as a line joining the base of a shape to its top. In parallelograms and trapezia, it can be drawn in more than one position.

 4 The area of a trapezium is the sum of the two parallel sides, multiplied by height, divided by 2.

In algebra, this is $A = \frac{1}{2}(a + b)h$ or $\frac{(a + b)h}{2}$.

This formula often appears on the information page at the front of your test booklet.

It doesn't matter which parallel side you choose to be a and which you choose as b.

 2 To calculate the area of a parallelogram, multiply base by height.

In algebra, this is $A = bh$.

3 The area of a triangle is *base multiplied by height, divided by 2*.

In algebra, this is $A = \frac{1}{2}bh$ or $\frac{bh}{2}$.

For some triangles, the perpendicular height drops down from the **apex** to a point **outside** the base. Simply continue the line of the base so the height can meet it at **right angles**.

For right-angled triangles, either of the sides making the right angle can be chosen as the base – the other is automatically the height.

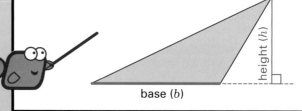

HELP!

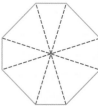

Quite often, there will be more information on a diagram than you need. Always make sure you identify the base and perpendicular height correctly. For example, the area of this rhombus isn't 25 cm²!

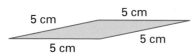

Level 7

You can calculate the areas of some polygons by treating them as compounds of other shapes. For example, this octagon can be seen as:

 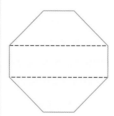

… a rectangle and two trapezia, or …   … a square with triangular corners removed, or …   … two sets of four identical triangles.

- All area calculations involving parallelograms, triangles and trapezia use the perpendicular height of the shape.

- Compounds of rectangles and the shapes covered on this page can be used to make any polygon.

Copy and complete

Copy these shapes. Mark and label b, h and a on them where appropriate, and write the correct area formulae underneath.

 2 mins

Sketch and label as many different triangles as you can with area 10 cm².

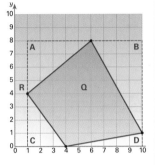

Questions and model answers

1 Calculate the area of this trapezium:

13 m, 13 m, 12 m, 20 m, 24 m

$$A = \tfrac{1}{2}(a+b)h = \tfrac{1}{2}(13+24) \times 12$$
$$= 37 \times 6 = 222 \, \text{cm}^2$$

Comments
Note that $\frac{1}{2} \times 12$ is easier to calculate, rather than $\frac{1}{2} \times 37$.

Comments
You could split Q into 4 triangles and a rectangle to calculate its area.

2 On a coordinate grid with x- and y-axes running from 0 to 10, plot the points (1, 4), (6, 8), (10, 1) and (4, 0). Join them in order to make a quadrilateral. Now draw a rectangle with corners at (1, 0), (1, 8), (10, 8) and (10, 0).

By removing triangles from this rectangle, find the area of the quadrilateral. Assume that the grid units are centimetres.

Area of $R = bh = 9 \times 8 = 72 \, \text{cm}^2$

Area of $A = \tfrac{1}{2}bh = \tfrac{1}{2} \times 5 \times 4 = 10 \, \text{cm}^2$

Area of $B = \tfrac{1}{2}bh = \tfrac{1}{2} \times 4 \times 7 = 14 \, \text{cm}^2$

Area of $C = \tfrac{1}{2}bh = \tfrac{1}{2} \times 3 \times 4 = 6 \, \text{cm}^2$

Area of $D = \tfrac{1}{2}bh = \tfrac{1}{2} \times 6 \times 1 = 3 \, \text{cm}^2$

$A + B + C + D = 10 + 14 + 6 + 3 = 33 \, \text{cm}^2$

Area of $Q = R - (A + B + C + D)$
$$= 72 - 33 \, \text{cm}^2 = 39 \, \text{cm}^2$$

Now try these!

1 Find the area of each shape.

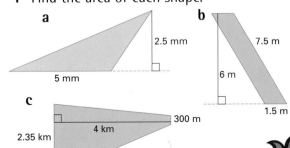

a 2.5 mm, 5 mm

b 7.5 m, 6 m, 1.5 m

c 300 m, 4 km, 2.35 km

2 A triangle has area 40 cm² and base length 10 cm. What is its perpendicular height?

Level 7

Draw a coordinate grid with x- and y-axes running from -10 to 10. Plot the points (1, 0), $(-2, 5)$, (6, 5), (3, 0), (8, 3), $(8, -5)$, $(3, -2)$, $(6, -7)$, $(-2, -7)$, $(1, -2)$, $(-4, -5)$ and $(-4, 3)$. Join them in order to make a 12-sided cross. Assuming that the grid units are centimetres, find its area.

Circle calculations

 The perimeter of a circle is called its circumference.

Other parts of a circle also have names.

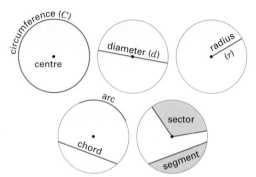

Note that the diameter of a circle is twice as big as its radius: $d = 2r$.

2 The circumference is not a whole number times the diameter.

In every circle, the circumference is just over 3 times the diameter. This number is very important in mathematics and has been given a special name, π (pi is the Greek letter P). So the circumference formula is $C = \pi d$.

The decimal value of π can never be written down exactly. The first five decimal places are 3.14159 . . .

You will usually be told what rough value to use in a question (often 3.14), or you may use the $\boxed{\pi}$ key on your calculator.

The value of π is also very close to $3\frac{1}{7}$ $\left(\frac{22}{7}\right)$, so you may be asked to use that.

 If you know the circumference of a circle, you can find its diameter.

Just reverse the formula: $d = \dfrac{C}{\pi}$.

4 Calculating the area of a circle also involves π.

This shows a square with a circle drawn inside it. The side length of one of the small squares is the same as the radius r of the circle, so its area is r^2. The quarter-circle takes up about $\frac{3}{4}$ of this square, so the area of the whole circle must be about $3r^2$. In fact, the area of the circle is just slightly more than this: $A = \pi r^2$.

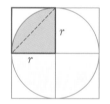

 If you know the area of a circle, you can find its diameter.

Just reverse the formula: $r = \sqrt{\dfrac{A}{\pi}}$ and $d = 2r$.

You can then go on to find the circumference, if required.

 HELP!

If you're doing a question where you have to use a value calculated in an earlier part, store it in your calculator, so you don't have to type it in again.

 The distance travelled by a wheeled vehicle is related to the circumference of the wheels.

Whenever a wheeled vehicle rolls along the ground; for every revolution of a wheel, the vehicle travels a distance equal to the circumference of the wheel. (Remember that 1 revolution = 1 whole turn.)

Level 7 To calculate the length of an arc, just multiply the circumference by the fraction of the circle in the question. For example, a 60° arc is $\frac{60}{360}$ or $\frac{1}{6}$ of the circumference. Use the same technique to find the area of a sector.

 **Remember**

- **The circumference of a circle is π times its diameter.**

- **The area of a circle is π times the square of its radius.**

Work-out!

Copy and complete

Draw a circle (more than one if necessary). Name and label all the parts.

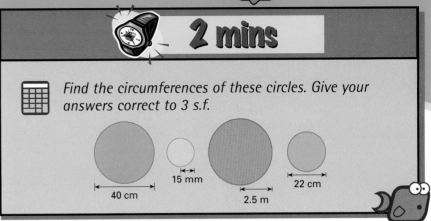

2 mins

Find the circumferences of these circles. Give your answers correct to 3 s.f.

40 cm

15 mm

2.5 m

22 cm

Questions and model answers

1000 ÷ 1.55 = 645.16 . . .,
so 645 complete revolutions are made.

1 Calculate the circumference and area of a circle with diameter 15 cm. Give your answers correct to 1 d.p.

$C = \pi d = 3.14159 \ldots \times 15 = 47.1238 \ldots$
$= 47.1$ cm to 1 d.p.
$A = \pi r^2 = 3.14159 \ldots \times 7.5^2 = 3.14159 \ldots$
$\times 56.25 \ldots = 176.7145 \ldots = 176.7$ cm^2 to 1 d.p.

Comments

If 3.14 is used as an approximation for π, C = 47.1 cm as before, but A = 176.6 cm² to 1 d.p.

Comments

If the answer had come out to be 645.6, you would not round up to 646, as the question asks for complete revolutions.

3 The circumference of a circular inspection cover is 1 m. What is its area? Give your answer correct to 3 significant figures.

Diameter $d = \frac{C}{\pi} = \frac{1}{3.14159\ldots} = 0.3183 \ldots$ m
Radius $r = \frac{1}{2}d = 0.1591 \ldots$ m
Area $A = \pi r^2 = 3.14159 \ldots \times (0.1591 \ldots)^2$
$= 0.07957 \ldots$ m$^2 = 0.0796 \ldots$ m^2, to 3 s.f.

2 The wheels on my bike are 50 cm in diameter. How many complete revolutions do the wheels make if I cycle exactly 1 km? Use 3.1 as an approximation for π.

$C = \pi d = 3.1 \times 50 = 155$ cm $= 1.55$ m
1 km = 1000 m.

Comments

If you prefer to answer in cm², multiply the answer in m² by 10 000, to give 796 cm². Alternatively, use C = 100 cm at the start and work the whole question in cm.

Now try these!

Give your answers correct to 3 s.f. when necessary.

1 A can of beans is 8 cm in diameter. The label wraps around the can once, with a 2 cm overlap.

  a How long is the label?

  b The label is 14 cm high. What is the area of the label?

2 If Samantha rides 500 m on her bike, the wheels make 400 revolutions. What is the diameter of her wheels?

3 A synchrotron is a device for accelerating protons to nearly the speed of light. A typical synchrotron contains a metal tube 50 km long, bent into a circle and surrounded by powerful electromagnets.

  a Calculate the diameter of the synchrotron.

  b What area of land is enclosed by the synchrotron?

Solid shapes

1 Solid shapes are also known as three-dimensional, or 3D, shapes.

Solids that have no curved surfaces are known as **polyhedra**. A polyhedron has flat **faces** that are all polygons. Faces join along a straight **edge**. Edges meet at a **vertex**.

This cube has ... ... 6 faces ... ... 12 edges ... ... 8 vertices.

2 Prisms are solids with the same cross-section all the way through.

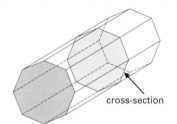

cross-section

Cuboids and cylinders are types of prism.

 3 Pyramids have a base and an apex.

Tetrahedra and cones are types of pyramids.

apex

base

4 All polyhedra have a net.

The net is how the faces look when laid out flat.

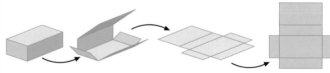

Always label measurements on a net when possible. The surface area of a polyhedron is the area of its net.

 5 Another way of describing a 3D shape on paper is with a plan and elevations.

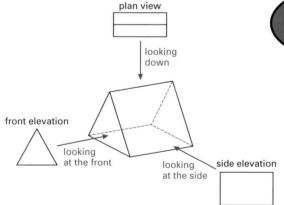

plan view

looking down

front elevation

looking at the front

looking at the side

side elevation

HELP!

When making an isometric drawing, try hard to think about which parts of your shape are hidden.
Never try to draw a triangular prism, like this, for example!

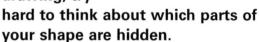

 6 You can draw a realistic picture of a solid shape on an isometric grid.

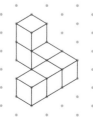

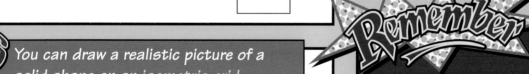
Remember

- **Prisms have the same cross-section all the way through.**

- **Pyramids 'come to a point'.**

- **3D shapes can be represented on 2D paper using nets, plans and elevations, or an isometric drawing.**

Copy and complete

This shape is called an <u>octahedron</u>.
Copy the picture, then write down the number of faces, edges and vertices it has.

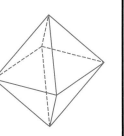

2 mins

Draw plan/elevation diagrams for a cylinder and a square-based pyramid.

Question and model answer

1 A prism has this shape as its cross-section (all measurements are in cm).
The length of the prism is 10 cm.

 a Draw a net of the prism.
 b Draw a plan and elevations.

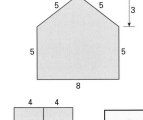

a

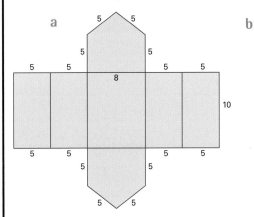

b

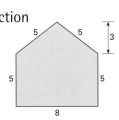

Comments

b Mark measurements on plan/elevation diagrams where possible.

Now try these!

1 This net folds up to make a cube.
When the cube is made up, the face labelled 'B' is on the bottom, touching the table.
Mark with a 'T', the face that will be on top.

2 A prism has this triangle as its cross-section, and is 8 cm long.

 a Draw a net of the prism.
 b Draw a plan and elevations.
 c Calculate the surface area of the prism.

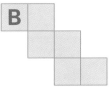

13 cm
5 cm
12 cm

3 Copy and complete this table for prisms with different cross-sections.

cross-section of prism	faces	edges	vertices
triangle	5	9	6
quadrilateral			
pentagon			
hexagon			
octagon			
n-sided polygon			

Volume and capacity

1 *Volume is the amount of space an object takes up.*

Volume is measured in cubic units such as cubic centimetres (cm³), cubic metres (m³), etc.

2 **Cuboids have three pairs of rectangular faces.**

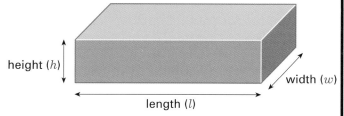

To calculate the volume of a cuboid, multiply together width, length and height.
In algebra, $V = lwh$.

3 *Cubes are cuboids too, but have their own extra formulae.*

To find the volume of a cube, cube one of the edges:
$V = e \times e \times e = e^3$.
To find the edge length if you know the volume, cube root it: $e = \sqrt[3]{V}$.

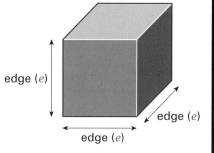

edge (e)

edge (e)

edge (e)

4 *If you know the volume of a cuboid and two of the edges, you can work out the other edge.*

Just divide the volume by the product of the known sides.
In algebra, make l, w or h the subject of the volume formula: $l = \dfrac{V}{wh}$ or $w = \dfrac{V}{hl}$ or $h = \dfrac{V}{lw}$.

5 *Capacity is the amount a 3D hollow shape can hold.*

Capacity units are litres (l), millilitres (ml), etc.
Capacity units and cubic units are equivalent:

1 cm³ = 1 ml
1000 cm³ = 1 l
1 m³ = 1000 l

HELP!

People often underestimate how many smaller volume units you need to make up the larger ones.

There are 10 × 10 × 10 = 1000 mm³ in 1 cm³, and 100 × 100 × 100 = 1 000 000 cm³ in 1 m³!

Level 7

To find the volume of a prism, multiply the area of its cross-section (or end) by the length or height.

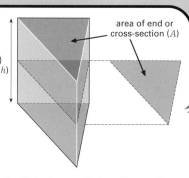

length (l) or height (h)

area of end or cross-section (A)

In algebra, $V = Al$ or Ah. This formula is often given at the start of the paper.

Remember

- **The volume of a cuboid = width × length × height.**

- **Cubic volume units and capacity units are equivalent. 1 cm³ = 1 ml.**

Copy and complete

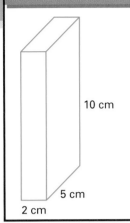

10 cm

5 cm

2 cm

This cuboid's volume is 100 cm³.
Copy it, then sketch and label as many different cuboids as you can that have the same volume.

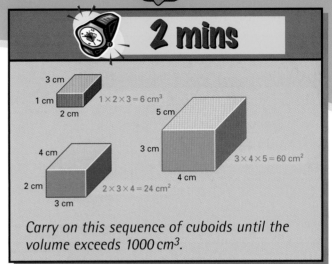

2 mins

3 cm
1 cm
2 cm
$1 \times 2 \times 3 = 6$ cm³

5 cm
3 cm
4 cm
$3 \times 4 \times 5 = 60$ cm²

4 cm
2 cm
3 cm
$2 \times 3 \times 4 = 24$ cm²

Carry on this sequence of cuboids until the volume exceeds 1000 cm³.

Questions and model answers

1 a A foam camping mat, when unrolled, is a cuboid 2 m by 60 cm by 8 mm. What is its volume?

b The mass of 1 cubic metre of the foam is 15 kg. What is the mass of one mat?

a 2 m = 200 cm and 8 mm = 0.8 cm.
Volume = $200 \times 60 \times 0.8 = 9600$ cm³.

b 9600 cm³ = $\frac{9600}{1\,000\,000}$ m³ = 0.0096 m³.
Weight = $0.0096 \times 15 = 0.144$ kg or 144 g.

Comments

a The calculation is impossible unless the units are matched first.

b It's important to remember the relationships between the volume units. If you can't remember them, make sure you can work them out.

2 A tub of ice cream is a cuboid whose base is 16 cm by 10 cm.

The tub contains 1 litre of ice cream.
To what depth is the tub filled?

1l = 1000 cm³. The depth (height) of the cuboid of ice cream is $\frac{1000}{16 \times 10} = 6.25$ cm.

Comments

Any cuboid can be treated as a prism with a rectangular cross-section. Here $A = 160$ cm².

3 A cube with volume 1 m³ has edges 1 m long. How long are the edges of a cube with volume 2 m³? Give your answer to the nearest centimetre.

$\sqrt[3]{2} - 1.2599 \ldots$ m = 1.26 m to 2 d.p.

Now try these!

1 What is the volume of a cube with 99 cm edges?

2 A CD jewel case is 14 cm by 12.5 cm by 1 cm. A cassette tape case is 6.8 cm by 10.8 cm by 1.4 cm. Which takes up the most volume, and by how much?

3 The learner's pool at my local swimming baths is 25 m by 20 m, and is filled to a depth of 90 cm.

a How much water is in the pool when it is full? Give your answer in litres.

b What does this amount of water weigh (1 litre of water weighs 1 kg)?

4 The petrol tank of a car is a cuboid 50 cm long, 40 cm wide and 25 cm high. The petrol gauge reads full when the tank contains 47 l. How deep is the fuel when the gauge just reads full?

Similar shapes: enlargements

1 Similar shapes are identical apart from their size.

Shapes like this are said to be **enlargements** of each other.

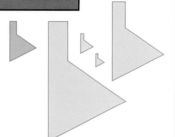

2 Enlargements use a scale factor to describe how they change the size of a shape.

If the scale factor of an enlargement is 2, the lengths in the image are twice those in the object. All angles in the shape are unchanged, but all lengths are multiplied by 2. This means that the area is multiplied by $2^2 = 4$. Always square the scale factor for the increase in area.

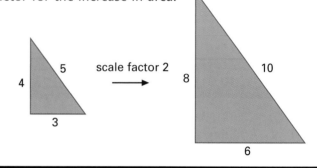

3 Like rotations, enlargements have a centre, which is fixed.

Everything else 'explodes' away from the centre.
To find the centre, connect corresponding points on the object and image. The centre is where the lines meet.

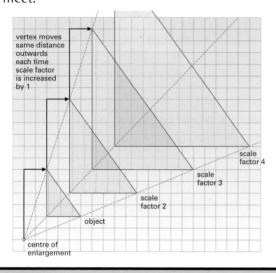

4 Solid shapes can be enlarged too.

The second cuboid is an enlargement of the first, with scale factor 3. This means its surface area is $3^2 = 9$ times bigger, and its volume is $3^3 = 27$ times bigger. Always cube the scale factor for the increase in volume.

Level 7

Enlarging with a **fractional** scale factor makes the image smaller than the object (and closer to the centre of enlargement).

HELP! **It's easy to get a vertex out of place when drawing enlargements. Pick one point and make certain it's right, then work from there, creating the enlargement. You can then check the other points against the centre.**

Remember

- **Similar shapes are enlargements of each other.**

- **Enlargements multiply all lengths in a shape by the scale factor. There is always a fixed point, the centre of enlargement.**

Copy and complete

Mark all the measurements and angles on the enlargement.

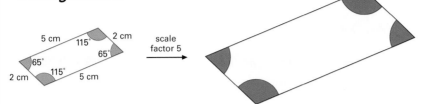

scale factor 5

Are all squares similar to each other?

Are all triangles similar? If not, which ones are?

Make a list of shapes that are always similar.

Question and model answer

2 a Draw a coordinate grid with x- and y-axes from -10 to 10.

Draw an object shape by joining the following points: $(1, -3) \rightarrow (4, -3) \rightarrow (1, -6) \rightarrow (0, -4) \rightarrow (1, -4) \rightarrow (1, -3)$.

Draw an image shape by joining the following points: $(-5, 9) \rightarrow (7, 9) \rightarrow (-5, -3) \rightarrow (-9, 5) \rightarrow (-5, 5) \rightarrow (-5, 9)$.

b What is the scale factor of the enlargement?

c Write down the coordinates of the centre of enlargement.

a

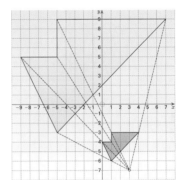

b 4

c $(3, -7)$

Comments
Notice how connecting the matching points on the object and image leads back to the centre.

Now try these!

1 a Draw a coordinate grid with x- and y- axes from -10 to 10.

Draw an object by joining the following points: $(1, 2) \rightarrow (4, 2) \rightarrow (1, 3) \rightarrow (1, 2)$. Label this shape **P**.

b Enlarge **P** with scale factor 2, centre $(9, 2)$. Label this shape **Q**.

c Enlarge **P** with scale factor 6, centre $(3, 4)$. Label this shape **R**.

d If **Q** is the object and **R** is the image, what is the scale factor of the enlargement, and where is the centre?

e What do you notice about the three centres of enlargement?

2 These two cuboids are mathematically similar.

a Calculate the volume of the smaller cuboid.

b How many small cuboids would it take to equal the volume of the larger cuboid?

c What is the scale factor of the enlargement?

d What are the measurements of the larger cuboid?

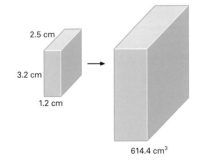

2.5 cm

3.2 cm

1.2 cm

614.4 cm^3

Bar charts and pictograms

1 In a bar chart, the height of a bar is used to show the frequency of a data item.

For example, you could display the information in this frequency table using a bar chart.

hours per night	number of pupils
0	3
1	4
2	10
3	16
4	13
5	7
6	4

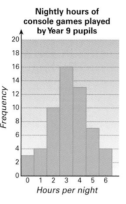

Nightly hours of console games played by Year 9 pupils

2 A pictogram is a chart where sets of pictures show the frequencies.

The pictures must be the same size and equally spaced. There must be a **key**, to tell the reader how many data items one picture is worth. This pictogram shows the same information as the bar chart on the left.

Hours played per night

Key: ☺ = 4 pupils

3 Bar charts can be used to compare two sets of data.

A **double bar chart** shows the bars from both sets side-by-side. This makes it easy to compare frequencies.

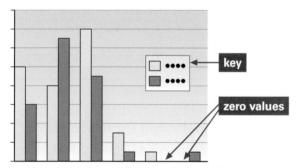

key

zero values

A **stacked bar chart** shows one set of bars on top of the other. This makes it easier to compare fractions of the total.

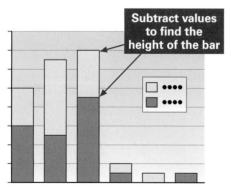

Subtract values to find the height of the bar

HELP!

When getting information from a bar chart, look carefully at the frequency scale. It may have been chosen to mislead you. Look at this, for example:

There isn't really much difference

Bettaco way ahead of opposition!

between the two companies, but the chart makes it look as if Bettaco has much higher sales than its nearest rival.

Remember

- In a bar chart, frequency is represented by the height of a bar.
- In a pictogram, the number of pictures for each item is proportional to the frequency.
- Two or more sets of data can be shown on a bar chart.

Copy and complete

Copy the phrases that go together with a well-drawn pictogram.

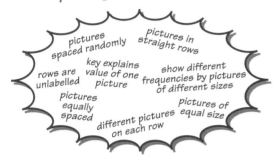

pictures spaced randomly

pictures in straight rows

rows are unlabelled

key explains value of one picture

show different frequencies by pictures of different sizes

pictures equally spaced

different pictures on each row

pictures of equal size

---

 2 mins

Joanne gathered some information for a survey on car colours. She tallied the colours as she walked round a large car park.

white	✔✔✔ ✔✔✔ ✔✔✔ I
red	✔✔✔ ✔✔✔ ✔✔✔ ✔✔✔ III
blue	✔✔✔ III
green	IIII
others	✔✔✔ ✔✔✔

Draw a frequency table of her results.

Question and model answer

1 This bar chart shows the number of words in text messages sent by pupils in two tutor groups, one in Year 8 and one in Year 9.

Use the chart to construct a frequency table.

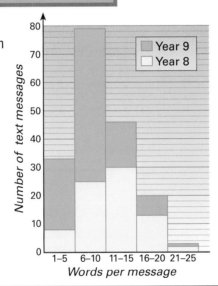

words per message	total	Year 8	Year 9
1–5	33	8	33 − 8 = 25
6–10	79	25	79 − 25 = 54
11–15	46	30	46 − 30 = 16
16–20	20	13	20 − 13 = 7
21–25	3	2	3 − 1 = 2

Now try this!

1 This table shows the results of a survey on how many pets people had.

Number of pets per person	girls	boys
0	18	11
1	15	24
2	27	16
3	5	2
4	1	0

a Draw a double bar chart to illustrate this data. On graph paper, use a scale of 2 cm = 5 people for the frequency axis. Choose your own scale for the 'number of pets' axis.

b Calculate the total number of people who took part in the survey.

c Calculate the total number of pets owned by all the people who took part.

d Calculate the mean number of pets per person (see page 84 for information on the mean).

Pie charts

 1 A *pie chart* illustrates frequencies by dividing a circle up into *sectors*.

Pie charts are good for showing what **fraction of the total** one item takes up. For example, in this pie chart, the red sector obviously has about $\frac{1}{4}$ of the total frequency.

 2 When drawing a pie chart, calculate how many degrees are needed to represent *one* item.

Then calculate the numbers of degrees for each sector and check that they total 360°. For example, if you were illustrating the data for 20 people, then each person would need $360° \div 20 = 18°$ of the pie chart.

 3 When reading a pie chart, you may be asked what fraction some of the sectors represent.

These are some of the angles you might need to recognise.

fraction of chart	angle	
$\frac{1}{2}$	180°	
$\frac{1}{3}$	120°	
$\frac{2}{3}$	240°	
$\frac{1}{4}$	90°	
$\frac{3}{4}$	270°	
$\frac{1}{6}$	60°	
$\frac{1}{8}$	45°	

 4 You may be asked to calculate the frequency for one or more sectors.

If you have the **total frequency**, divide this by 360. This tells you how many items are represented by 1° (it will probably be a fraction). Store this value in your calculator, especially if it's a complicated decimal. Then you can multiply by the number of degrees in each sector. Check that your answers add up to 360°.

If you have the frequency for **one of the sectors**, divide by the number of degrees in the sector, then carry on as above.

 5 You might be asked to compare two pie charts.

Remember that you can only compare angles on the two charts if they have the same total frequency. Otherwise, a bigger angle might actually mean fewer items!

HELP!

Don't confuse angle and frequency. Just because a sector contains a right angle, this doesn't mean it represents 90 items. That depends on the total frequency.

- **Each sector on a pie chart represents one entry in a frequency table.**
- **The angle for each sector is proportional to the frequency.**

Work-out!

Copy and complete

Label each sector with the correct angle.

 2 mins

Write down as many simple fractions as you can. Write down the pie chart angle that matches each fraction.

Question and model answer

1 The table gives the area of land used for different purposes on a farm.

land use	area in hectares
wheat	540
barley	410
woodland	250
total	1200

Draw a pie chart to illustrate this information.

1 hectare of land is represented by $360° \div 1200 = 0.3°$ on the pie chart.

The angles are: wheat, $540 \times 0.3° = 162°$; barley, $410 \times 0.3° = 123°$; woodland, $250 \times 0.3° = 75°$.

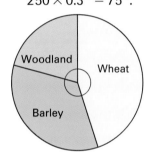

Comments

Check the angle total: $162° + 123° + 75° = 360°$.

Now try these!

1 Sanjeev asked people how they find out what's on TV. This table gives his results:

	frequency
listings magazine (e.g. Radio Times)	43
newspaper (national or local)	36
teletext/Internet	11

a How many people did Sanjeev ask?
b Draw a pie chart to show his results.

2 Employees at a factory are paid one of four salaries:

salary code	amount per year
A	£40 000
B	£30 000
C	£20 000
D	£10 000

This pie chart shows how the workforce is split up between the salary codes.

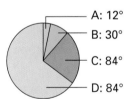

A: 12°
B: 30°
C: 84°
D: 84°

a Copy and complete this table:

salary code	number of employees	total salaries per year
A	2	2 × £40 000 = £80 000
B	5	
C	14	
D	39	
Total		

b Draw a pie chart to show how the factory's salary bill (the total above) is split between the different salary codes.

Scatter diagrams

1 A scatter diagram is used to investigate a possible link between two sets of data items.

One set is plotted on the horizontal axis and the other on the vertical axis. Patterns in the points plotted show if there is a link.

3 Scatter diagrams are useful for spotting 'rogue' data items.

On a correlated scatter diagram, any points that don't follow the trend 'stick out'.

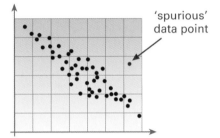

'spurious' data point

2 If the sets of data items are linked, they are said to be *correlated*.

These diagrams show different types of correlation. If the data items are **positively correlated**, this means that as one goes up, so does the other.

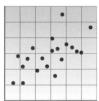

Strong positive correlation   Weak positive correlation

If, when one value goes up, the other goes down, the items are **negatively correlated**.

Uncorrelated (no link)   Strong negative correlation

If the points are scattered randomly over the graph, there is **no correlation**.

Level 7

Often, a **line of best fit** is added to a scatter diagram. This has two uses:

- to show the correlation more clearly
- to make predictions about other data items.

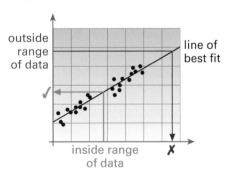

outside range of data   line of best fit

inside range of data

The line has to 'follow the trend' of the data points. This is quite easy to do 'by eye'.

To make predictions using the line, simply read from one scale to the other as on any graph.

Note that you can only use the line for this purpose **within the range of the data** or slightly outside it.

HELP!

You may occasionally have to plot two points with the same values. Don't just ignore the second one – put a ring round the existing point, for example.

Remember

- **Positive correlation on a scatter diagram means that as one value goes up, so does the other.**

- **Negative correlation on a scatter diagram means that as one value goes up, the other goes down.**

- **Random patterns of data points mean that there is no correlation.**

Copy and complete

Draw sketch graphs showing the following types of correlation:

a strong positive
b weak negative
c weak positive
d none
e strong negative.

 **2 mins**

Do you think there are any 'rogue' data points in the scatter diagram from question 1 below?

Explain your answer.

Question and model answer

1 This table shows the marks ten pupils got in the mental test (out of 30), and the marks they got on Papers 1 and 2 combined (out of 120).

mental	10	13	16	18	21	22	24	28	29	30
P1 + P2	23	62	80	30	51	77	56	84	100	87

a Draw a scatter diagram. Use a scale of 2 cm = 20 marks on the 'P1 + P2' axis, and 2 cm = 5 marks on the 'mental' axis.
b Describe the correlation, if any, between the marks.

a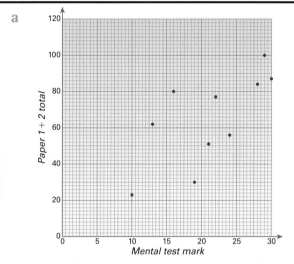

b The two marks are weakly positively correlated.

Comments

a *The scales have been chosen to make the correlation more obvious.*
b *The marker would accept any answer that describes the same idea accurately.*

Now try this!

1 This table shows the annual salaries earned by ten people, and the size of the mortgage loan they have for their houses. The figures are in thousands of pounds.

salary (£000)	12	15	20	22	26	28	33	35	44	50
mortgage (£000)	52	45	55	64	56	76	80	100	92	98

a Draw a scatter diagram. Use a scale of 2 cm = £10 000 on the 'Salary' axis, and 2 cm = £20 000 on the 'Mortgage' axis.

b Describe the correlation, if any, between the salaries and mortgages.

 Level 7

c Add a line of best fit to the scatter diagram above. Use it to estimate the mortgage for someone earning £40 000.

Mode and median

 1 *Averages are used to give a 'typical' value for a set of data.*

There are three main types of average: the mode, median and mean.

 2 *The mode is the most common item in a set of data.*

When data has been placed into groups, the group with the highest frequency is called the **modal group**. You can spot the mode easily on a bar chart, because it has the highest bar.

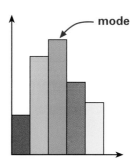
mode

 3 *Features of the mode are:*

- It always has to be the same as one of the data values.

- There may be more than one mode if there's a 'tie for first place'.

- It's the only average that exists for data that isn't numerical (i.e. not numbers).

> Find the mode of this set of numbers: 3, 4, 2, 7, 3, 2, 4, 4, 5, 3. There are three 3s and three 4s, so 3 and 4 are the modes.

 4 *The median is the middle value in a set, when all the numbers are arranged in order.*

If you have an even number of data items, the median is halfway between the two in the middle.

median
↓

5 *Features of the median are:*

- It is equal to one of the data values, **unless** there are an even number of data items and the two middle values are different.

- There is only one median for any data set.

- When the data is arranged in order, there are the same number of them 'to the left' of the median as there are 'to the right'.

> Find the median of this set of numbers: 3, 4, 2, 7, 3, 2, 4, 4, 5, 3. Arrange the numbers in order: 2, 2, 3, 3, 3, 4, 4, 4, 5, 7. The median is halfway between the fifth and sixth positions, which are a 3 and a 4. So the median is 3.5.

HELP!

Many people get the mode and median muddled up. Try remembering it like this:

Mode = Most

Median = Middle

 Remember

- **The mode is the item in a set of data with the highest frequency – the one that there's 'most of'.**

- **The median is the middle value when the items are arranged in order.**

Copy and complete

Write down the modal item or items on this pictogram.

A ☀ ☀
B ☀ ☀ ☀ ☀
C ☀ ☀ ☀ ☀ ☀ ☀ ☀ ☀
D ☀ ☀ ☀ ☀ ☀ ☀ ☀
E ☀ ☀ ☀ ☀ ☀ ☀ ☀ ☀
F ☀ ☀ ☀ ☀ ☀

Write down the median of these items.

130 135 137 137 140 141 142 142 142 146 151

2 mins

This frequency table shows the shoe sizes of all Year 9 pupils at Sandworth school.

Find the modal and median shoe sizes.

shoe size	frequency
4	6
5	11
6	21
7	62
8	53
9	42
10	15

Question and model answer

1 The bar chart shows the weights of a group of pupils.

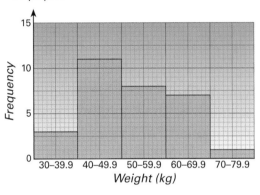

Find: **a** the modal weight group
b the group containing the median weight.

a 40–49.9 kg
b 50–59.9 kg

Comments

a This group has the highest bar.

b There are 30 pupils altogether. The first two groups contain 14 pupils between them. The median is between the 15th and 16th, and so is in the next group.

Now try these!

1 a Write down five numbers that have a mode of 10 and a median of 20.

b Write down six numbers that have a mode of 10 and a median of 20.

2 a Cherie rolls a die ten times and writes down her scores:

2 5 2 5 6 2 1 5 4 2

i What is her modal score?

ii What is her median score?

b Aziz says:

I added 50 to all of Cherie's numbers.

i What is the mode of Aziz's numbers?

ii What is the median of his numbers?

c Sherona says:

I multiplied all of Cherie's numbers by 10.

i What is the mode of Sherona's numbers?

ii What is the median of her numbers?

d Cherie rolls her die once more. When she adds the new score to her list, the mode and median do not change. Write down the number she scored on this roll.

Mean and range

  The **mean** is the most frequently used average.

 DATA → Add up all the data items to find their total → Divide the total by the number of items → MEAN

 Features of the mean are:

- Any set of data has only one mean.
- The mean does not have to be equal to any of the data values.

Find the mean of this set of numbers: 3, 4, 2, 7, 3, 2, 4, 4, 5, 3. The total is 37. There are ten numbers, so the mean is $37 \div 10 = 3.7$.

 In a frequency table, multiply the data values by the frequencies to find the totals.

A group of 100 people were asked how many musical instruments they could play.

number of instruments per person	frequency	total number of instruments
0	67	$0 \times 67 = 0$
1	25	$1 \times 25 = 25$
2	8	$2 \times 8 = 16$

mean $= 41 \div 100 = 0.41$

The **range** is not an average, but tells you how 'spread out' the data is.

It is simply the difference between the smallest and largest data items.

Find the range of this set of numbers: 3, 4, 2, 7, 3, 2, 4, 4, 5, 3. The smallest number is 2 and the largest is 7. So the range is $7 - 2 = 5$.

 HELP!

If you're finding a mean from a frequency table, be sure to use the right figures! For example, in the question in box 3, don't add $0 + 1 + 2 = 3$, then divide by 3 to get the answer 1. Even worse is calculating the total, 41, correctly, then dividing this by 3 to get a 'mean' of 13.7 instruments per person! Always check that your answer is reasonable.

 You can compare two sets of data using their means and ranges.

Suppose these are the results of testing two brands of light bulb.

	mean lifetime (hours)	range (hours)
brand A	550	50
brand B	610	220

Brand B lasts longer on average, but is not as **consistent** as Brand A. Some Brand B bulbs could fail after a very short time. This might not be acceptable!

Level 7

When data is in groups, you need to estimate the mean. To do this, you use mid-interval values (MIVs). You assume that all the items in a group are exactly in the middle of the group.

 **Remember**

- **The mean is the total of the data items divided by the total frequency.**
- **For grouped data, the mean can only be estimated.**
- **The range is the difference between the smallest and largest values in a set of data.**

Copy and complete

Finish each line with an algebraic expression.

The mean of 2 numbers x and y is _____ .

The mean of 3 numbers x, y and z is _____ .

The mean of 4 numbers w, x, y and z is _____ .

2 mins

Write down as many groups of three whole numbers as you can, that have a mean of 3.

Which group has the largest possible range?

Question and model answer

1 Two machines, M_1 and M_2, are supposed to fill drink bottles with exactly 330 ml of liquid. The factory manager is satisfied if the mean volume is within 1 ml of this, and the range of volumes is 10 ml or less. Ten bottles from each machine were tested. These were the results.

M_1	332	338	344	335	333	337	333	341	334	332
M_2	329	320	324	329	338	311	334	328	345	347

a Calculate the mean and range for each machine.

b Comment on the performance of both machines.

a

	mean (ml)	range (ml)
M_1	335.9	12
M_2	330.5	36

b M_1 has a small enough range, but its mean volume is much too high. M_2's mean volume is within the manager's limit, but the range shows that it is very inconsistent. Both machines have faults and will need adjusting.

Comments

a All the volumes are 300, plus a two-digit number. You can find the mean of the two-digit numbers, then add it to 300. It saves time and you're less likely to make a mistake.

Now try this!

1 Max plays snooker. He keeps a record of all the breaks he makes that are over 50 points. Here is his list:

64	52	72	51	104	68	65

a What is the mean of these scores?

b What is the range?

c Max's next over-50 break increases the mean to 75. What was the break score?

d What is the new range?

2 100 adults were asked how many children they had. This bar chart gives the results:
Calculate the mean number of children.

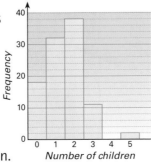

Number of children

Level 7

People browsing in a music shop were asked how many CDs they thought they owned.

This table gives the results:

number of CDs	frequency
0–50	67
51–100	313
101–200	344
201–300	158
301–500	78
501–1000	24

Calculate an estimate of the mean number of CDs owned.

Theoretical probability

 1 **Things that happen according to the laws of chance are called events.**

Events have **outcomes**. Each outcome of a chance event has a **probability**. Probabilities are numbers between 0 and 1 that describe how likely an outcome is to happen. You can show probabilities on a probability scale.

```
              even
impossible    chance              certain
   |----|----|----|----|----|----|----|----|----|----|
   0   0.1  0.2  0.3  0.4  0.5  0.6  0.7  0.8  0.9   1
                      (½)
```

Probabilities are written as **fractions**, **decimals** or **percentages**. Avoid using phrases like '2 to 1', '1 chance in 6', etc.

 2 **You can often calculate probabilities by analysing an event mathematically.**

A probability that has been calculated in this way is called a **theoretical probability**.

Theoretical probabilities are easy to calculate if the outcomes are **equally likely** (have the same probability), for example, flipping a fair coin has two outcomes, head and tail, with equal probabilities.

This is written $P(\text{head}) = P(\text{tail}) = \frac{1}{2}$.

The two outcomes are also exclusive because they can't both happen at once. When outcomes are exclusive, their probabilities must add up to 1.

3 **Some probabilities that are not equal can be calculated, too.**

On this spinner, the angle for the black section is $120°$.
That's $\frac{1}{3}$ of $360°$, so $P(\text{black}) = \frac{1}{3}$.

4 **You can use probability to predict the results of experiments.**

For example, the probability of rolling a six with an ordinary die is $\frac{1}{6}$. So if you roll a die 60 times, you would expect to roll a six about 10 times.
Each roll is one **trial** of the event.

For each outcome,
expected frequency = probability $\times$ number of trials.

 5 **Use a possibility space diagram to work out probabilities that depend on two sets of outcomes.**

This diagram shows the outcomes for rolling two dice (one red, one blue) and adding the scores together.

		blue die					
		1	2	3	4	5	6
red die	1	2	3	4	5	6	7
	2	3	4	5	6	7	8
	3	4	5	6	7	8	9
	4	5	6	7	8	9	10
	5	6	7	8	9	10	11
	6	7	8	9	10	11	12

There are 36 cells in the table. Each outcome has probability $\frac{1}{36}$.
Four of the cells score a 5, so $P(5) = \frac{4}{36} = \frac{1}{9}$, or 0.11 to 2 d.p.

HELP!

Don't jump to conclusions about probabilities. Just because an event has, say, four outcomes, this doesn't mean the probabilities are all $\frac{1}{4}$! Look carefully to see if the outcomes are equally likely, and if not, work out what 'controls' them (e.g. with a spinner, it's the turning angle for each section).

Remember

- **Events have outcomes. Each outcome has a probability.**

- **The sum of all the probabilities for exclusive outcomes is 1.**

Copy and complete

Expected frequency = _____ × _____ .

If the probability of winning a game is w,

then $1 - w$ is _____ .

2 mins

Copy this spinner.

Write numbers on it so that the probability of scoring 3 is $\frac{1}{2}$ and the probability of scoring an even number is $\frac{1}{3}$.

Question and model answer

1 a Calculate P(yellow) and P(red) for this spinner.

b If the spinner is given 60 spins, how many times do you expect each colour to come up?

a $P(\text{yellow}) = \frac{7}{12}$ and $P(\text{red}) = \frac{5}{12}$.

b Yellow: $\frac{7}{12}$ of 60 = 7 × 5 = 35.
Red: $\frac{5}{12}$ of 60 = 5 × 5 = 25.

2 Ailsa has two dice like this, that show the numbers 1–4 (you score the number that's in contact with the table).

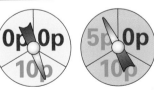

a Draw a possibility space diagram to show the possible results when she rolls both dice and adds the scores together.

b Which score is most likely?

c What is the probability of scoring this number?

d If she rolled the dice 200 times, how many times would you expect her to score 7?

a

		1st die		
	1	2	3	4
1	2	3	4	5
2	3	4	5	6
3	4	5	6	7
4	5	6	7	8

(2nd die labels rows 1–4)

b 5

c $\frac{4}{16} = \frac{1}{4}$

d $P(7) = \frac{2}{16} = \frac{1}{8}$
$\frac{1}{8}$ of 200 = 25 times

Now try this!

1 These two spinners are spun together. You win the total amount of money shown on the spinners.

a Draw a possibility space diagram for the spinners.

b What is the probability of winning 10p?

c What is the probability of winning nothing?

d If you spun the spinners 90 times, how many times would you expect to win nothing?

2 a A bag contains 5 white, 10 yellow and 15 black counters. You take a counter at random from the bag. Calculate the probability of obtaining each colour.

b Suppose you picked a black counter. You take another from the bag at random. What is the probability that you will get another black?

3 A set of Lotto balls contains all the numbers 1, 2, 3 . . . up to 49. What is the probability that the first ball the machine selects will have the digit '1' on it?

Experimental probability

 1 **Sometimes you have to *estimate* probabilities.**

This happens when you can't use a mathematical method to calculate them. For example, suppose you want to know the probability that a drawing pin will finish point-up or point-down when you drop it. There's nothing about the drawing pin or the way you drop it that can help you to calculate the probabilities.

 2 **To estimate probabilities, you need to gather data perhaps by doing an experiment.**

In the drawing pin example, this means dropping a pin a number of times and recording the results.

Suppose that in 100 trials, this happened:

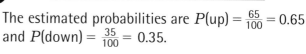

direction of point	frequency
up	65
down	35
total	100

The estimated probabilities are $P(\text{up}) = \frac{65}{100} = 0.65$ and $P(\text{down}) = \frac{35}{100} = 0.35$.

$$\text{Estimated probability} = \frac{\text{frequency of outcome}}{\text{total frequency}}$$

 3 **If you repeat an experiment, you'll get slightly different results.**

If you dropped the drawing pin another 100 times, you probably wouldn't get 65 and 35 again, but something similar. It would make sense to combine the two sets of 100 into one large sample of data.

The more trials you do, or the larger your data sample, the more accurate the estimated probabilities should be.

4 **An object, such as a coin or die, can be altered to become biased instead of fair.**

A **fair** die is one that lands on all six numbers with equal probability.

A **biased** die is one that looks fair, but doesn't have equal probabilities for all the outcomes.

 5 **You can estimate probabilities from existing data.**

Suppose a magazine has 25 000 male readers and 15 000 female readers. The total readership is 40 000, so the probability that a reader picked at random is male is $\frac{25\,000}{40\,000} = \frac{5}{8}$.

 HELP!

Suppose you have these results of 120 rolls of a die.

score	1	2	3	4	5	6
frequency	24	21	18	16	22	19

You might think that this shows there is something wrong with the die, as the frequencies 'should' all be 20. In fact, this amount of variation from the calculated frequencies is quite normal. It would have to be much more uneven than this to make you worry that the die might be biased.

 **Remember**

- **Probabilities have to be estimated when there isn't a clear mathematical way of calculating them.**
- **To estimate probabilities, carry out a number of trials or use information already available.**

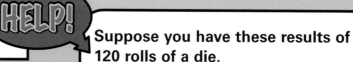

Work-out!

Copy and complete

Experimental probability

= _____ ÷ _____

A biased coin is one that

....

2 mins

When a die was rolled 600 times, these were the scores.

Score	1	2	3	4	5	6
Frequency	190	208	113	89	0	0

This is the net of the die.

Copy it and add numbers to the faces, either as dots or digits.

This is the net of an ordinary die, for comparison.

Question and model answer

1 At a fête, 55 raffle tickets are bought by men and 78 by women. There is a single prize.

   a What is the probability that a man will win? Give your answer to 2 d.p.

   b What is the probability that a woman will win?

a 55 + 78 = 133 tickets are sold.
   $P(\text{man}) = \frac{55}{133} = 0.41$ to 2 d.p.

b $P(\text{man}) + P(\text{woman}) = 1$,
   so $P(\text{woman}) = 1 - 0.41 = 0.59$ to 2 d.p.

Comments

It could happen that answer b has an incorrect second decimal place due to a rounding error. You could check that $P(\text{woman}) = \frac{78}{133}$ gives the same answer.

Now try this!

1 A word game uses cards with letters on them. Some letters are on more cards than others. This table gives the numbers of letters in the pack.

letter	frequency	letter	frequency
A	4	N	2
B	1	O	4
C	1	P	1
D	2	Q	1
E	5	R	2
F	1	S	2
G	2	T	3
H	1	U	3
I	4	V	1
J	1	W	1
K	1	X	1
L	2	Y	1
M	2	Z	1

   a How many cards are there in the pack?

   b The pack is shuffled and you pick a card at random. What is the probability that you will get a vowel (A, E, I, O or U)?

   c What is the probability you will get a consonant (not a vowel)?

2 This spinner is spun 120 times. The results are:

area	frequency
X	42
Y	78

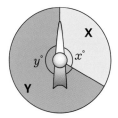

Use this information to work out an estimate of angle X and angle Y.

Using and applying maths

1 Throughout the tests, there are many times when you will have to *solve a problem.*

Problem solving is different from answering a straightforward question, where it's obvious what techniques you will use. Problems involve thinking more deeply. You usually have to make some decisions about how to tackle the problem.

2 You will need to choose the correct mathematics.

Unlike most ordinary questions, some problems may need you to use two or more branches of maths.

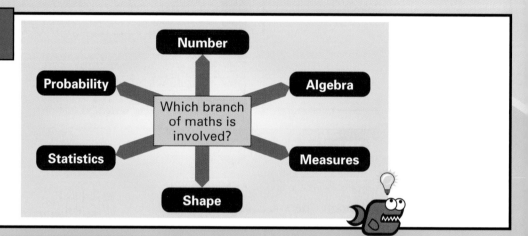

- Number
- Probability
- Algebra
- **Which branch of maths is involved?**
- Statistics
- Measures
- Shape

3 Make sure you have enough information to tackle the problem.

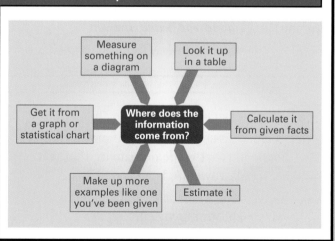

- Measure something on a diagram
- Look it up in a table
- Get it from a graph or statistical chart
- **Where does the information come from?**
- Calculate it from given facts
- Make up more examples like one you've been given
- Estimate it

4 Most test questions guide you through solving the problem.

The parts of the question usually lead you through to the solution. Some problems may have more than one correct solution.

5 Even in more straightforward questions, you will often be asked to *explain why* your answer is correct.

This is also 'using and applying' maths. If you have thought carefully about the question, the explanation should be obvious. There are two kinds of explanation:

- A purely mathematical explanation: 'the number is 3 because ten times the number was 30' is a simple example.

- A common-sense explanation: for example, 'The frequency is higher because people drink more hot drinks in winter'.

The decimal system, page 7

2 mins

Here are some possible answers:
0.0022, 0.022, 0.22, 2.2, 22, 220, 2200,
0.0202, 0.202, 2.02, 20.2, 202, 2020,
0.2002, 2.002, 20.02, 200.2, 2002, etc.

The first number is: 'nought point nought nought nought two two'.

Now try these!

1 a 3440

 b 16 016

 c 425 500 000

2 3 904 000: three million, nine hundred and four thousand

3 a i Mark ii Cara iii Leah

 b 6 places

The four rules, page 9

2 mins

1 × 2	2	98
2 × 3	6	94
3 × 4	12	88
4 × 5	20	80
5 × 6	30	70
6 × 7	42	58
7 × 8	56	44
8 × 9	72	28
9 × 10	90	10

1 × 3	3	97
2 × 4	8	92
3 × 5	15	85
4 × 6	24	76
5 × 7	35	65
6 × 8	48	52
7 × 9	63	27
8 × 10	80	20
9 × 11	99	1

Now try these!

1 a 951 b 1566

 c 48 192 d 562

2 a $(4 + 2) \times 10 - 6 = 54$

 b $4 + 2 \times 10 - 6 = 18$ (none needed)

 c $4 + 2 \times (10 - 6) = 12$

 d $(4 + 2) \times (10 - 6) = 24$

Calculation techniques, page 11

2 mins

0	7
1	14
2	28
3	56
4	112
5	224
6	448
7	896
8	1792
9	3584

10	7168
11	14 336
12	28 672
13	57 344
14	114 688
15	229 376
16	458 752
17	917 504
18	1 835 008

Now try these!

1 a 2085, 1170, 3255

 b 996, 81, 2166

 c 39 900, 21 600, 63 300

 d 17 955, 9720, 28 485

e 15 960, 8640, 25 320

f 399, 216, 633

2 a 2520 b 3150 c 126

Powers and roots, page 13

2 mins

number	square	cube
1	1	1
2	4	8
3	9	27
4	16	64
5	25	125
6	36	216
7	49	343
8	64	512
9	81	729
10	100	1000

Now try these!

1 a 4^4 b 22.1^3 c 10^9

2 11, 121, 1331, 14 641, 161 051

3 a 1 953 125 b 100 000 000

 c 2.56 d 0.015625

 e 53 f 12

 g 7.071 to 3 d.p. h 1.644 to 3 d.p.

4 $\boxed{?} = 6$

Working with negative numbers, page 15

2 mins

(1×-36), 2×-18, 3×-12, 4×-9, 6×-6, 9×-4, 12×-3, 18×-2, 36×-1.

NB integers are positive or negative whole numbers.

Now try these!

1

+	0	(7)	(−12)
(−8)	−8	−1	−20
(−10)	−10	−3	−22
−12	(−12)	−5	(−24)

2 a −12 b 45

 c −32 d 11

3 a 64 b 20 and −20

4 $-4 \times 7 = -28$; $13 - -14 = 27$.
 27 is much larger.

Calculators: functions, brackets and memory, page 17

2 mins

To 3 decimal places, the numbers should be:
10, 3.317, 2.078, 1.754, 1.660, 1.631,
1.622, 1.619, 1.618, 1.618, 1.618, 1.618 . . .

Now try these!

1 40 2 882

3 25.4 4 6

5 9 6 −343

7 1.55 8 2.56

Rounding, estimating and checking, page 19

2 mins

The possible answers are given below.

type of rounding	rounded number
nearest thousand (1 s.f.)	4000
nearest hundred (2 s.f.)	3800
nearest ten (3 s.f.)	3850
nearest whole number (4 s.f.)	3848
nearest tenth (1 d.p.)	3847.6
nearest hundredth (2 d.p.)	3847.57
nearest thousandth (3 d.p.)	3847.569

Now try these!

1 a 89.4 b 276 000

 c 0.0331 d 1.23

 e 2700

2 a $(0.57 + 0.82) \times 0.25 + 1.3 = 13.3475$

 $13.3475 - 1.3 = 12.0475$

 $12.0475 \div 0.25 = 48.19$

 $48.19 - 0.82 = 47.37$. Wrong!

 b 1.6475

 c She typed 13 instead of 1.3.

Level 7

a $20 \times 2 \times 0.7 \div 20 = 1.4$

b 2.1505. The estimate is reasonable, about $\frac{2}{3}$ of the accurate answer.

Equivalent fractions, page 21

2 mins

$\frac{1}{4} = \frac{2}{8} = \frac{3}{12} = \frac{4}{16} = \frac{5}{20} = \frac{6}{24} = \frac{7}{28} = \cdots$

$\frac{3}{10} = \frac{6}{20} = \frac{9}{30} = \frac{12}{40} = \frac{15}{50} = \frac{18}{60} = \frac{21}{70} = \cdots$

Now try these!

1 a = 6, b = 25, c = 50, d = 40, e = 4, f = 12, g = 9, h = 20.

2 a $\frac{3}{4}$

 b $\frac{12}{25}$

 c $\frac{9}{49}$

3 $\frac{7}{18} \left(\frac{14}{36}\right)$, $\frac{5}{12} \left(\frac{15}{36}\right)$, $\frac{1}{2} \left(\frac{18}{36}\right)$, $\frac{5}{9} \left(\frac{20}{36}\right)$, $\frac{7}{12} \left(\frac{21}{36}\right)$

Improper and mixed fractions, page 23

2 mins

$\frac{5}{2}, \frac{8}{3}, \frac{11}{4}, \frac{14}{5}, \frac{17}{6}, \frac{20}{7}, \frac{23}{8}, \ldots$

8, $5\frac{1}{3}$, 4, $3\frac{1}{5}$, 4, $2\frac{2}{3}$, 2, . . .

Now try these!

1 A = Y, B = V, C = Z, D = U, E = X, F = W

2 a $\frac{26}{7} = 3\frac{5}{7}$

 b $\frac{34}{9} = 3\frac{7}{9}$

 c $\frac{18}{5} = 3\frac{3}{5}$

3 $3\frac{3}{5}, 3\frac{5}{7}, 3\frac{7}{9}$ (the fractional parts are $\frac{189}{315}, \frac{225}{315}, \frac{245}{315}$)

Fraction calculations, page 25

2 mins

$\frac{3}{8} + \frac{2}{3} = 1\frac{1}{24}$ $\frac{2}{3} - \frac{3}{8} = \frac{7}{24}$

$\frac{3}{8} - \frac{2}{3} = -\frac{7}{24}$ $\frac{3}{8} \times \frac{2}{3} = \frac{1}{4}$

$\frac{3}{8} \div \frac{2}{3} = \frac{9}{16}$ $\frac{2}{3} \div \frac{3}{8} = 1\frac{7}{9}$

Now try these!

1 a $\frac{5}{6}$ b $\frac{7}{12}$

   c $1\frac{1}{2}$ d $4\frac{1}{10}$

   e $3\frac{43}{50}$

2 a $\frac{2}{3} \times \frac{1}{4} = \frac{1}{6}$

   $\frac{2}{3} \times \frac{3}{10} = \frac{1}{5}$

   $\frac{2}{3} \times 1\frac{1}{2} = 1$

   b $3\frac{1}{5} \times \frac{4}{9} = 1\frac{19}{45}$

   $3\frac{1}{5} \times \frac{5}{8} = 2$

   $3\frac{1}{5} \times 2\frac{2}{5} = 7\frac{17}{25}$

3 a $\frac{2}{3} \div \frac{1}{4} = 2\frac{2}{3}$

   $\frac{2}{3} \div \frac{3}{10} = 2\frac{2}{9}$

   $\frac{2}{3} \div 1\frac{1}{2} = \frac{4}{9}$

   b $3\frac{1}{5} \div \frac{4}{9} = 7\frac{1}{5}$

   $3\frac{1}{5} \div \frac{5}{8} = 5\frac{3}{25}$

   $3\frac{1}{5} \div 2\frac{2}{5} = 1\frac{1}{3}$

Percentages, fractions and decimals, page 27

2 mins

The decimals are $0.\dot{1}4285\dot{7}$, $0.\dot{2}8571\dot{4}$, $0.\dot{4}2857\dot{1}$, $0.\dot{5}7142\dot{8}$, $0.\dot{7}1428\dot{5}$, $0.\dot{8}5714\dot{2}$

They contain the same cycle of digits: they just start with a different digit each time.

Now try these!

1 a 0.3, 30 %   b 0.09, 9 %

   c 0.08, 8 %   d 0.55, 55 %

   e 0.625, $62\frac{1}{2}$ %   f $0.\dot{0}\dot{9}$, $9\frac{1}{11}$ % or 9.09%

2 a 0.9   b 0.35

   c 0.06   d 0.375

   e 1.1   f 2.35

3 0.235, $\frac{6}{25}$ (0.24), $\frac{1}{4}$ (0.25), 27 % (0.27), $\frac{2}{7}$ ($0.\dot{2}8571\dot{4}$)

Fractions or percentages of an amount, page 29

2 mins

$\frac{1}{2}$ = £15, $\frac{1}{3}$ = £10, $\frac{1}{5}$ = £6,

$\frac{1}{10}$ = £3, $\frac{1}{12}$ = £2.50

1 % = £0.30, 5 % = £1.50, 25 % = £7.50, $2\frac{1}{2}$ % = £0.75, 99 % = £29.70.

Now try these!

1 £1020

2 200 red, 300 orange.

3 640 g

4 £7480

5 £57.75

£34.034 . . . = £34.03 to the nearest penny.

Ratios, page 31

2 mins

$m \times n = 1$, always.

Now try these!

1 a 3   b 1.5   c 10   d 75   e 24

2 Cars : trucks : buses = 1200 : 600 : 300

3 3 m = 300 cm. 300 ÷ 15 = 20.

   The scale is 1 : 20.

4 12 km = 12 000 m = 1 200 000 cm.

   1 200 000 ÷ 50 000 = 24 cm

Amounts in proportion: conversion graphs, page 33

2 mins

| X | 4.8 | 7.2 | (12) | (15) | (30) | 42 |
| Y | (2) | (3) | (5) | 6.25 | 12.5 | (17.5) |

Now try these!

 1a   2.4 : 1

b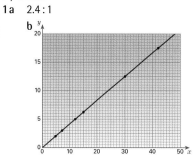

c The exact value is 4.1666 . . ., so an answer around 4.2 is good.

2 a 22.5 kg cement and 7.5 kg water

   b 75 kg.

x	−2	−1	0	1	2
x^2	4	1	0	(1)	4
$3x$	−6	−3	0	(3)	6
$x^2 - 3x$	10	4	0	(−2)	−2

3 £2.40

Substitution, page 35

2 mins

Now try these!

1 a 4   b 1   c 4   d 1.5

2 a $C = \frac{t + 30}{20}$

   b For 3 minutes, $t = 180$.

   $C = \frac{180 + 30}{20} = \frac{210}{20} = 10.5$ pence

3 a $n + 1$ b $2n$ c $10 - 4n$ d $\frac{100}{n}$

Simplifying expressions, page 37

2 mins

uv and vu are like terms, because $uv = vu$, whatever the values of u and v. The order in which you multiply numbers doesn't matter.
u/v and v/u are not like terms because $u \div v$ and $v \div u$ always give different answers unless $u = v$. The order in which you divide numbers does matter.

Now try these!

1 a $3j + 7k$ b $2e - d$

   c $-3y + 6$ (or $6 - 3y$)   d $2w + 16$

   e $b^2 + b$ f $7T + 26$

   g $7x + 3y$ h $17g + 3h$

2 a $N + 1$ b $N + 2$

   c $N + N + 1 + N + 2$ d $3N + 3$

   e N is a whole number, so $3N$ is a multiple of 3. If you add 3 to a multiple of 3, you get another multiple of 3.

   Another way to prove it is to notice that $3N + 3$ is an expanded version of $3(N + 1)$. If N is a whole number, so is $N + 1$, and 3 times that must be a multiple of 3.

a $(x + 5)(x + 2) = x(x + 2) + 5(x + 2)$
$= x^2 + 2x + 5x + 10 = x^2 + 7x + 10$.

b $(x + 6)(x - 1) = x(x - 1) + 6(x - 1)$
$= x^2 - x + 6x - 6 = x^2 + 5x - 6$.

Solving equations and transforming formulae, page 39

2 mins

$x - 2 = 0$, $x - 1 = 1$, $x + 1 = 3$, $x + 2 = 4$, $2x - 2 = 2$, $2x - 1 = 3$, $2x = 4$, $2x + 1 = 5$, $2x + 2 = 6$, $3x - 2 = 4$, $3x - 1 = 5$, $3x = 6$, $3x + 1 = 7$, $3x + 2 = 8$, etc.

Now try these!

1 a $x = 3$ b $x = -1$

   c $x = 2.5$ d $x = 1.5$

   e $x = 2$

2 a $y = \frac{x - 4}{2}$

   b $w = \frac{P}{2} - l$ or $\frac{P - 2l}{2}$

3 a When $x = 4$, $x^2 - 4x = 0$
   When $x = 5$, $x^2 - 4x = 5$, so the solution is between them.

   b $x = 4.45$

Coordinates and functions, page 41

2 mins

Some examples are:

$y = x + 1$, $y = 2x + 1$, $y = 3x + 1$, etc.

$y = 1 - x$, $y = 1 - 2x$, $y = 1 - 3x$, etc.

$y = x^2 + 1$, $y = x^3 + 1$, $y = x^4 + 1$, etc.

Now try these!

1 For the function $x \rightarrow 2x - 3$ with input set $\{-1, 0, 1, 2, 3, 4\}$:

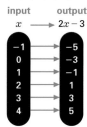

1b $y = 2x - 3$

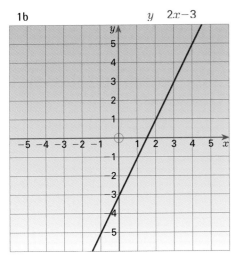

2 a

b $y = x - 2$

Straight-line graphs, page 43

2 mins

The gradient has to be 2 to be parallel to $y = 2x$, so the equation has to be $y = 2x + c$.
At the point (5, 3), $x = 5$ and $y = 3$.
If $y = 2x + c$, then $3 = 2 \times 5 + c$,
or $3 = 10 + c$, so $c = -7$.
So the equation is $y = 2x - 7$.

Now try these!

1

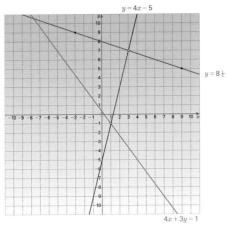

d (3, 7)

Level 7

Point of intersection is (1, −1).

Multiples, factors and primes, page 45

2 mins

Some possible denominators are 2, 4, 5, 8, 10, 16, 20, 25, 32, 40, 50, 64, 100, . . .
They all have only 2, 5 or both as prime factors.

Now try these!

1 a {1, 2, 3, 6, 9, 18}; 2×3^2
 b {1, 2, 4, 8, 16}; 2^4
 c {1, 2, 4, 11, 22, 44}; $2^2 \times 11$
 d 53 is prime; 1, 53
 e {1, 2, 3, 6, 13, 26, 39, 78}; $2 \times 3 \times 13$
 f {1, 3, 9, 11, 33, 99}; $3^2 \times 11$
 g {1, 2, 4, 7, 8, 14, 16, 28, 56, 112}; $2^4 \times 7$
 h {1, 5, 23, 115}; 5×23
2 a LCM = 48 ; HCF = 4
 b LCM = 315; HCF = 5
 c LCM = 120; HCF = 2

Number patterns and sequences, page 47

2 mins

Some possible answers are:

5, 10, 15, 20, . . . (add 5)
5, 10, 16, 23, . . . (add 5, 6, 7, etc.)
5, 10, 17, 22, . . . (add 5, 7, 9, etc.)
5, 10, 14, 17, . . . (add 5, 4, 3, etc.)
5, 10, 20, 40, . . . (multiply by 2)
5, 10, 20, 35, . . . (add 5, 10, 15, etc,)
5, 10, 15, 25, . . . (as for Fibonacci)

Now try these!

1 a . . ., 17, 20, 23 **b** . . ., 4, −1, −6,
 c . . ., 2.55, 2.8, 3.05 **d** . . ., 40, 52, 66
 e . . ., 224, 448, 896 **f** . . ., 216, 343, 512
2 The term−to−term rule is 'add 6', and the fifth term is 32.
3 9, 1.9, 1.19, 1.119, 1.1119, . . .
 The terms get closer and closer to $1.\dot{1} = 1\frac{1}{9}$.

Sequences and formulae, page 49

2 mins

1, 4, 27, 256, 3125, 46 656, 823 543,
16 777 216, 387 420 489, 10 000 000 000.

Now try these!

1 a 6, 10, 14, 18, 22, . . .
 b 1, −2, −5, −8, −11, . . .
 c 0, 5, 10, 15, 20, . . .
 d 3, 9, 19, 33, 51, . . .
2 a Green: $T = 3n + 3$ Pink: $T = 2n + 7$
 b 303 green, 207 pink.

Metric and imperial units, page 51

2 mins

1 cm = 0.4 in	1 cm = 0.0$\dot{3}$ ft or 1 m = 3.3 ft
1 m = 1.1 yd	1 km = 0.63 mi
1 g = 0.036 oz	1 kg = 2.2 lb
1 kg = 0.16 st	1 tonne is about 1 ton
1 l = 1.75 pt	1 l = 0.22 gal

Now try these!

1

(20 kg)	0.02 t	20 000 g
1550 m	(1.55 km)	1 550 000 mm
(285 ml)	28.5 cl	0.285 l

2 48.6 kg to 1 d.p.
3 A 50 pence piece weighs 15 g.
 a $20 \times 15 = 300$ g
 b $1000 \div 15 = 66.\dot{6}$: 67 is the nearest whole number.
4 5.13 km

Level 7

Lowest: $5.5 \times 3.5 = 19.25$ cm²
Highest: $6.5 \times 4.5 = 29.25$ cm²

Time calculations, page 53

2 mins

365−day year: 31 536 000 seconds
366−day year: 31 622 400 seconds
Sidereal year (365 days, 3 hours, 56 minutes 4 seconds): 31 550 164 seconds

Now try these!

1 6:47:44
2 42 minutes

Level 7

192.5 km

Time-based graphs, page 55

2 mins

160 km

Now try these!

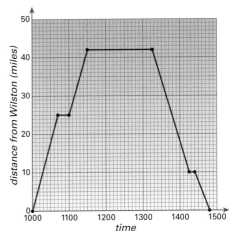

Level 7

1000−1045: 25 miles in $\frac{3}{4}$ hour = $33\frac{1}{3}$ mph
1100−1130: 17 miles in $\frac{1}{2}$ hour = 34 mph
1315−1415: 32 miles in 1 hour = 32 mph
1424−1445: 10 miles in 21 min or 0.35 hour = 28.57. . . mph

The second section, from Conisham to Fortley Castle, is the fastest.

Angle facts, page 57

2 mins

This should check itself — if your total is in the range 177°−183° for the triangles, and 356°−364° for the angles at a point, you've measured accurately enough.

Now try these!

1 $a = 57°$ (angle sum of large triangle)

$b = 122°$ (vertically opposite 122°)

$c = 122°$ (corresponding with b)

$d = 96°$ (angle sum of quadrilateral)

$e = 84°$ (adjacent to d)

$f = 58°$ (adjacent to c)

$g = 96°$ (corresponding to d)

$h = 84°$ (corresponding to e)

Note there are other ways of finding many of the angles.

2 No. The angles total 370°, which is impossible for a quadrilateral.

3

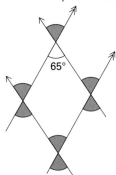

Symmetry and congruence, page 59

2 mins

The results will depend on what you tried. Try to get a 'feel' for how the position of the centre affects the position of the image.

Now try these!

1 a Reflection in the line $y = 3$.

  b Rotation, 180° about the origin (0, 0).

  c Reflection in the line $x = 2$.

  d Rotation, 90° anticlockwise about (3, −2).

3 a No lines of symmetry
   rotational symmetry order 2.

  b 3 lines of symmetry
   rotational symmetry order 3.

  c No lines of symmetry
   rotational symmetry order 5.

  d 4 lines of symmetry
   rotational symmetry order 4.

Triangles and quadrilaterals, page 61

2 mins

kite: scalene/congruent or isosceles/different

trapezium: scalene/different

isosceles trapezium: scalene/different

parallelogram: scalene/congruent

rhombus: isosceles/congruent

rectangle: right-angled/congruent

square: right-angled, isosceles/congruent

Now try these!

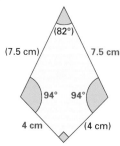

2 Angle $X = 60°$, angle $Y = 82°$, angle $Z = 38°$.

3

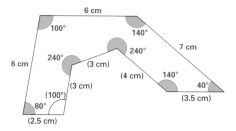

Polygons, page 63

2 mins

a	15°	yes	(360° ÷ 15° = 24)
b	30°	yes	(360° ÷ 30° = 12)
c	150°	no	(360° ÷ 150° = 2.4)
d	45°	yes	(360° ÷ 45° = 8)
e	50°	no	(360° ÷ 50° = 7.2)
f	120°	yes	(360° ÷ 120° = 3)
g	135°	no	(360° ÷ 135° = 2⅔)
h	6°	yes	(360° ÷ 6° = 60)

Now try these!

1 The total of the given angles
  = 48° + 132° + 80° + 63° = 323°
  The angle sum of a pentagon = 540°
  The unmarked angle is 540° − 323° = 217°

2 a 24 sides means 24 − 2 = 22 triangles.
   Angle sum = 22 × 180° = 3960°.

  b 3960 ÷ 24 = 165°

  c 180° − 165° = 15°.

3 180° − 140° = 40° (one exterior angle).
  360° ÷ 40° = 9. The polygon is a nonagon.

4 The angle sum of a quadrilateral is 360°.
  So $2x + x + x + 9x + 100 = 360°$.
  Simplifying, $13x + 100° = 360°$,
  and $13x = 260°$.
  Therefore, $x = 20°$.

Area: rectangles and compounds, page 65

2 mins

width (cm)	0.5	1	2	3	4	5
length (cm)	20	10	5	3.3	2.5	2
width (cm)	6	7	8	9	10	15
length (cm)	1.7	1.4	1.25	1.1	1	0.7

Now try these!

1

length	width	area
(21 cm)	(35 cm)	735 cm²
(8 m)	(8 m)	64 m²
18 m	(4.5 m)	(81 m²)
(12.5 cm)	3.2 mm	(400 mm²)
12.5 km	(1.6 km)	(20 km²)

2

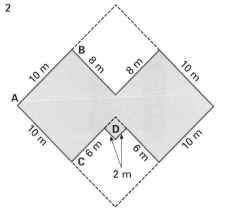

Area of A = 18² = 324 m².
Area of B = 8² = 64 m².
Area of C = 8² = 64 m².
Area of D = 2² = 4 m².
Area of shape = A − B − C + D = 324 − 64 − 64 + 4 = 200 m²

Area: parallelograms, triangles and trapezia, page 67

2 mins

The base and perpendicular height must multiply together to make 20. Any values that fit this will make a correct triangle.

Now try these!

1 Find the area of each shape.

  a 6.25 mm² b 9 m² c 5.3 km²

2 8 cm